Ready-To-Go Storytimes

Fingerplays,
Scripts,
Patterns,
Music,
and more

Gail Benton and Trisha Waichulaitis

Neal-Schuman Publishers, Inc.

New York   London

Published by Neal-Schuman Publishers, Inc.
100 Varick Street
New York, NY 10013

Printed and bound in the United States of America.

The paper used in this publication meets the minimum requirements of American National Standard for Information Sciences—Permanence of Paper for Printed Library Materials, ANSI Z39.48–1992 ⊗

Library of Congress Cataloging-in-Publication Data

Benton, Gail, 1950–
    Ready-to-go storytimes / Gail Benton, Trisha Waichulaitis.
        p.   cm.
    Includes bibliographical references and index.
        ISBN 1-55570-449-2 (alk. paper)
    1. Storytelling—United States. 2. Children's libraries—Activity programs—United States. I. Waichulaitis, Trisha, 1954– II. Title.
    Z718.3 .B46 2002
    027.62'51—dc21
                                                                    2002005806

CONTENTS

Kids will bask in these sunny desert stories.

    Desert Dash Outline   107
    The Welcome Song (*song #1 from CD*)   107
    Read-A-Loud (*book*)   108
    One Tarantula (*fingerplay*)   108
    Shady Hat (*flannel or magnetic story*)   108
    Five Little Coyotes (*flannel or magnetic story, song #7
        from CD*)   110
    Toad's Trip (*puppet story*)   111
    This Little Bird (*action song #8 from CD*)   112
    Matching (*parent and child activity*)   113
    The Stretch and Sit Song (*song #2 from CD*)   114
    Five Black and Shiny Crows (*flannel or magnetic story*)   114
    Come Hike in the Desert (*action song #9 CD*)   115
    Desert Dash Support Materials   117

4   BEACH PARTY   149

Kids will dive into these underwater adventure stories.

    Beach Party Outline   149
    The Welcome Song (*song #1 from CD*)   149
    Read-A-Loud (*book*)   149
    Little Hermit Crab (*magnetic story*)   150
    The Deep Blue Sea (*action song*)   150
    The Sand Castle (*fingerplay*)   151
    Goldfish (*flannel or magnetic story*)   151
    Gathering Seashells (*flannel or prop story*)   152
    Little Seashell (*fingerplay*)   153
    Matching (*parent and child activity*)   153
    The Stretch and Sit Song (*song #2 from CD*)   153
    Made at the Beach (*prop story*)   154
    We Dove in the Ocean (*action song #10 from CD*)   155
    Beach Party Support Materials   157

PREFACE

Ready-to-Go Storytimes: Fingerplays, Scripts, Patterns, Music, and More contains fun-filled, interactive thirty-minute storytime programs—complete from start to finish. Each of the six thematic chapters begins with an outline, is followed by a read-a-loud book suggestion, fingerplays, flannel/magnetic/prop or puppet story scripts, patterns with step-by-step instructions, songs, a parent-and-child matching activity, and activity sheet handouts. In addition, an accompanying CD—featuring more than a dozen songs, all written and sung by the authors—provides lively musical elements to use with every storytime. The book is packed with ready-to-use materials, so that each storytime can be created and implemented immediately, reducing the time busy professionals spend researching and developing storytimes. From the novice to the seasoned veteran, this user-friendly, all-inclusive book provides school and public librarians, preschool and elementary teachers, daycare providers, and home-school parents with the materials necessary to ensure storytime success.

Today's child lives and thrives in a visual world filled with movement, adventure, and excitement. Keeping up with this exciting pace is challenging storytellers and changing the face of traditional storytimes. We designed *Ready-to-Go Storytimes* for children eighteen months to five years of age, attending with a parent. Parents enjoy participating in their child's storytime and their hands-on involvement allows the storyteller a larger, yet more manageable crowd while also providing an opportunity for positive role modeling. While singing songs, reciting fingerplays, and taking part, firsthand, parents and children will not only have fun, but will take away a love for stories that will reach far beyond the storytime experience.

HOW TO USE THIS BOOK

While the various chapters may be used in random order, you will find that each storytime contains similar elements. They:

- offer a fun, two-word title and one-sentence tagline describing the theme that can be used to advertise your storytime (for example, Yum Yum, *Kids will eat up this feast of stories.*);
- begin with an outline explaining the entire storytime;
- provide a combination of quiet listening, story interaction, movement, and music—all designed to make your storytime flow effortlessly;
- supply a read-a-loud title to eliminate the need to search for related books;
- contain italicized step-by-step instructions, which immediately follow text;

- feature handy, graphic-quick guides to lead the storyteller easily through the event;
- present numbered directions and illustrations, a recipe-like format of materials, and pictures of puppets to assist in creating each fingerplay, story, and song;
- assist the storyteller by offering CD song lyrics with instructions for movement;
- expand the storytime experience, by providing instructions to create an interactive parent/child matching activity, specific to the theme; and
- deliver an activity sheet with printed instructions, making them ready for duplication.

Ready-to-Go Storytimes: Fingerplays, Scripts, Patterns, Music, and More brings a fresh, new approach to a reassuringly similar format. Each storytime follows the same plan, beginning with "The Welcome Song," which lets children know that storytime is beginning. Next, it's time to read a book; children are more attentive at the beginning of storytime. Original fingerplays, stories, and music are woven into the next fifteen minutes of the storytime experience. Then, an activity, which allows child and parent to work together, matching pictures or responding to simple questions, is introduced. This is followed by "The Stretch and Sit Song," which prepares children for the next story. Storytime ends with an interactive song, a coloring sheet, and activity handout, which reinforce the theme. Following this format each week not only provides continuity, but also allows children to find comfort in the familiar and a sense of security and belonging.

This winning format has evolved through the past eleven years as we continue to present successful storytimes to Arizona's youngest patrons and their parents. Our storytime not only introduces children to books and the library, but also plays an important part in early childhood brain development, building a foundation for learning. *Ready-to-Go Storytimes* provides this foundation by taking advantage of a child's natural curiosity and fun-loving spirit. It is our hope that you will enjoy presenting these stories, as much as your audience will enjoy watching them come alive.

ACKNOWLEDGMENTS

Many thanks to:

Jamie Abbott and Stephen Waichulaitis for putting our songs to music.

Pete Waichulaitis and Dale Benton for believing in us.

Our families, friends, and co-workers, for their support and love through this process.

City of Mesa Library for allowing us the opportunity to grow.

Jan Elliott, Arizona librarians, and teachers who encouraged us to put it in writing.

KEY OF ICONS

Fingerplay

Read-A-Loud

Parent and Child Activity

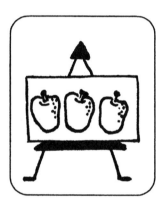

Flannel/Magnetic Story

Activity Sheet

Song

Prop Story

Yum Yum

THE WELCOME SONG

(*play CD song #1 to let children know you are ready to begin*)
Let's begin our story time, see a play, and hear a rhyme. Welcome mom and daddy too, they can sit right next to you. Songs to sing and books to see, you'll have fun each week with me.

READ-A-LOUD BOOK

Choose a book related to food; we recommend reading Strawberries Are Red *by Petr Horacek (Cambridge, Mass.: Candlewick Press, 2001).*

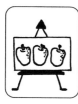

EGGS FOR BREAKFAST

(encourage children to join you in the following actions as you say, "give it a whack"—clap hands once; "hear it crack"—cup hand behind ear; "drop it in the middle"—clap hands once)

One morning I woke up early and no one was up yet. So I decided to make eggs for breakfast. I got out the griddle.

(point to flannel board, pretending it's the griddle)

I got out the eggs.

(hold up egg carton)

I picked up one egg and sang, "Give it a whack, hear it crack, drop it in the middle, one egg's fryin' on the griddle."

(hold up one finger, then place one egg on the board)

Just then, sis came into the kitchen rubbing her eyes.

(rub eyes)

She said, "I want one too!"

I picked up one egg and we sang, "Give it a whack, hear it crack, drop it in the middle, two eggs fryin' on the griddle."

(hold up two fingers, then place another egg on the board)

Here comes dad nodding his head. He likes his on toasted bread.

I picked up one egg and we sang, "Give it a whack, hear it crack, drop it in the middle, three eggs fryin' on the griddle."

(hold up three fingers, then place another egg on the board)

Here comes mom. She gave me a wink, "Looks good, I'll have one too!"

I picked up one egg and we sang, "Give it a whack, hear it crack, drop it in the middle, four eggs fryin' on the griddle."

(hold up four fingers, then place another egg on the board)

We're all here and it's time to eat!

To make as a flannel story: (see figure 1.1, page 13)

MAKING PIZZA

Stretch the dough.
> (*using both hands pretend to stretch dough*)

Spread the sauce.
> (*make spreading motion with open hand*)

Sprinkle on the cheese.
> (*wiggle fingers pretending to sprinkle cheese*)

Cook the pizza.
> (*with hand open and palm up pretend to slide pizza in oven*)

Cut the pizza.
> (*pretend to cut pizza*)

I'll have a big slice please!
> (*hold hand out, palm up*)

'CAUSE THEY'RE GRAPES!

> (*play song #3 from CD*)

You can stomp 'em, you can crush 'em, you can squeeze 'em, you can mush 'em,
> (*stomp feet, make crushing motion with hands, make squeezing motion, then rub hands together*)

but you're always gonna love 'em, 'cause they're grapes.
> (*hug self, then pretend to hold up a bunch of grapes*)

You can toss 'em, you can thread 'em, you can pop 'em, you can spread 'em,
> (*make tossing motion, make threading motion, pretend to pop a grape in mouth, then using index finger pretend to spread jam on opposite hand*)

doesn't matter how you eat 'em, 'cause they're grapes.
> (*shrug shoulders, then pretend to hold up a bunch of grapes*)

You can juice 'em, you can lick 'em, you can peel 'em, you can pick 'em,
> (*make squeezing motion, stick out tongue, pretend to peel a grape, then pretend to pick grapes*)

but for taste you just can't beat 'em, 'cause they're grapes.
> (*hug self, then make muscle*)

THE WIDE-MOUTH FROG FROM THE POND

(*mom off stage*)

"Time for supper! Hurry these flies aren't going to hang around all day."

(*note: the frog's mouth should open very wide whenever he talks*)

(*frog whining*)

"I don't want flies for supper again! I'm tired of flies, I'm going to see what other mothers give their babies to eat."

(*frog hops up and down, looking around*)

(*pig enters rooting around and snorting*)

(*frog*)

"Hi, I'm the wide mouth frog from the pond, what do you feed your babies?"

(*pig*)

"I feed my babies potatoes from the patch, they love them."

"Oh my, they'll be wanting their supper now, I've got to run."

(*pig exits*)

(*frog hopping up and down*)

"Mmmm potatoes, that sounds good."

"I'll ask my mom and dad to get me some for supper."

(*hen enters clucking and pecking*)

(*frog*)

"Hi, I'm the wide mouth frog from the pond, what do you feed your babies?"

(*hen*)

"I feed my babies corn from the fields, they eat it right up."

"Oh look at the time, they'll be wanting supper, I'd better fly."

(*hen exits*)

(*frog hopping up and down*)

"Mmmm, corn and potatoes, this is sounding better and better."

(*rabbit enters sniffing around*)

(*frog*)

"Hi, I'm the wide mouth frog from the pond, what do you feed your babies?"

(*rabbit*)

"I feed my babies lettuce from the garden."

"It's so good and it's suppertime right now, I'd better get hopping."

(*rabbit exits*)

(*frog hopping up and down*)

"Yum, yum, that's lettuce from the garden, corn from the fields, and potatoes from the patch. I guess I'd better find out where these places are."

(*snake slithers out*)

"SSSSSuppertimmmme."
>   (*frog*)

"Hi, I'm the wide mouth frog from the pond."
>   (*snake*)

"Sssso it ssseems."
>   (*frog*)

"What do you feed your babies?"
>   (*snake*)

"Welllll, let'ssss sssssee, we eat fliessss."
>   (*pause*)
>   (*frog*)

"Yes."
>   (*snake*)

"And micccce."
>   (*pause*)
>   (*frog*)

"Uh, huh."
>   (*snake*)

"But our favorite sssupper is wide mouth frogs from the pond, and it's just about ssssuppertime now!"
>   (*frog closes his mouth and trembles*)

"Oh, really, I think I hear my mama calling me from the pond right now . . . YIKES!"
>   (*frog exits quickly*)

> (*To use as a puppet story the following puppets are needed: frog, hen, snake, pig, and rabbit. If you don't own these puppets, follow the instructions, using the patterns provided on pages 14–37 to create your own.*)

FIVE GRAPES

One red grape
>   (*hold up one finger*)
is a little bitty snack.
>   (*hold thumb and index finger apart one inch*)
Two red grapes
>   (*hold up two fingers*)
are jelly for my bread.
>   (*use index finger and pretend to spread jelly on opposite palm*)
Three red grapes
>   (*hold up three fingers*)
are juice that's red.
>   (*pretend to hold cup*)

Four red grapes
  (*hold up four fingers*)
are dessert in my lunch.
  (*rub stomach with hand*)
Five red grapes
  (*hold up four fingers and thumb*)
are a great big bunch!
  (*hold hands out wide*)

MATCHING

A packet, with eight picture cards, is given to each child. The child and parent work together, listening to clues, then holding up the appropriate picture card. Make one packet for every child. Each packet will consist of eight pictures and a pocket to put them in.

To make picture cards—(see figures 1.21 and 1.22, pages 38 and 39) reproduce, color, and laminate the following pictures: bread, fish, spoon and fork, carrot, pretzel, ice cream cone, banana, and grapes.

To make a pocket: (see figure 1.23, page 40)

To introduce the activity, tell the children you will give them a clue and they will hold up the appropriate picture.

Clue suggestions:

1. Hold up the picture of something you use to make a sandwich *(bread)*.
2. Hold up the picture of something you catch before you eat it *(fish)*.
3. Hold up the picture of something a rabbit eats *(carrot)*.
4. Hold up the picture of something you use to eat with *(spoon and fork)*.
5. Hold up the picture of something that is salty *(pretzel)*.
6. Hold up the picture of something that is sweet and will melt if you don't eat it fast enough *(ice cream cone)*.
7. Hold up the picture of something that you have to peel before you eat it *(banana)*.
8. Hold up something that comes in a bunch and you must pull them off before you can eat them *(grapes)*.

THE STRETCH AND SIT SONG

(play song #2 from CD)
Let's stand up together. Now let's all touch our nose. Put our hands in the air high, bend down, and touch our toes. Let's stand up together. Now let's all touch our nose. Put our hands in the air high, bend down, and touch our toes. Now it's time to listen so sit right on the floor. Hands are in our laps now and we are ready for more.

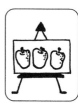

BEAR'S FEAST

(before you begin, place tree stump in middle of board)
Little Bear
(place smallest bear to right of tree stump, facing it)
and his mama
(place large bear to left of tree stump, also facing it)
woke up from their long winter's nap. Little Bear was hungry and his mama was hungry too. They came out of their bear den and looked around. In the clearing was the tree stump where they always had their feast. Little Bear hopped up onto the tree stump and sniffed around.
(place Little Bear on tree stump)
"Mama where's the food?" said Little Bear.
"We have to gather the food, Little Bear," said his mama. "Do you remember how good blueberries taste?" "I bet they're ripe." "Why don't you see if you can find them Little Bear?" So Little Bear hopped off the tree stump and ran into the woods.
(remove Little Bear from board)
Little Bear wasn't gone very long. When he came back he said, "Look Mama, blueberries!"
(place Little Bear on board and fish on tree stump)
(Mama bear says, laughing)
"No Little Bear, that's not a blueberry. That's a
(pause to allow children time to answer)
fish!"
"I'll try again," said Little Bear.
"This time go past the stream," said Mama.
"Okay Mama," said Little Bear as he ran back into the woods.
(remove Little Bear from board)
This time Little Bear was gone a little longer and when he returned he said,
"Look Mama, blueberries!"
(place Little Bear on board and acorn on tree stump)
(Mama bear says, laughing)

"No Little Bear, that's not a blueberry. That's an
> (*pause to allow children time to answer*)

acorn!"

"I'll try again," said Little Bear.

"This time go past the stream and around the big tree," said Mama.

"Okay Mama," said Little Bear as he ran back into the woods.
> (*remove Little Bear from board*)

This time Little Bear was gone longer than before and when he returned he said, "Look Mama, blueberries!"
> (*place Little Bear on board and apple on tree stump*)
> (*Mama bear says, laughing*)

"No Little Bear, that's not a blueberry. That's an
> (*pause to allow children time to answer*)

apple!"

"I'll try again," said Little Bear.

"This time go past the stream, around the big tree, and through the apple orchard," said Mama.

"Okay Mama," said Little Bear as he ran back into the woods.
> (*remove Little Bear from board*)

This time Little Bear was gone for a long time and when he returned he said,

"Look Mama, blueberries!"
> (*place Little Bear on board and orange on tree stump*)

(*Mama bear says, laughing*)

"No Little Bear, that's not a blueberry. That's an
> (*pause to allow children time to answer*)

orange!"

"I'll try again," said Little Bear.

"This time go past the stream, around the big tree, through the apple orchard, and under the orange tree," said Mama.

"Okay Mama," said Little Bear as he ran back into the woods.
> (*remove Little Bear from board*)

This time Little Bear was gone a really long time and when he returned he said, "Look Mama, I found the blueberries and Dad too!"
> (*place Little Bear and Dad on board together and blueberries on tree stump*)

"Yes Little Bear, those are blueberries, and you and Dad are just in time for dinner!" said Mama.

To make as a flannel story: (see figures 1.24, 1.25, 1.26, 1.27, and 1.28, pages 41 to 45)

To make as a magnetic story: (see figures 1.24, 1.25, 1.26, 1.27, and 1.28, pages 41 to 45)

FLIP-FLAP JACK

(before beginning, place the "pancake" near the top center of the board, and the waffle underneath it; place all other pieces randomly along edges of board; play song #4 from CD)
There was a man made of food. Made of food? Made of food!
There was a man made of food. His name was Flip-Flap Jack.
And he danced upon a table, a table, a table. He danced upon a table.
His name was Flip-Flap Jack.
His head was made of a pancake.
 (point to the pancake)
A pancake?
 (shrug shoulders and look questioningly)
A pancake! His head was made of a pancake. His name was Flip-Flap Jack.
His hair was made of whipped cream. Whipped cream?
 (shrug shoulders and look questioningly)
Whipped cream!
 (place whipped cream touching top edge of pancake)
His hair was made of whipped cream. His name was Flip-Flap Jack.
And he danced upon a table, a table, a table. He danced upon a table.
His name was Flip-Flap Jack.
His eyes were two blueberries. Blueberries?
 (shrug shoulders and look questioningly)
Blueberries!
 (place blueberries on pancake in eye position)
His eyes were two blueberries. His name was Flip-Flap Jack.
His nose was made of a strawberry. A strawberry?
 (shrug shoulders and look questioningly)
A strawberry!
 (place strawberry in nose position)
His nose was made of a strawberry. His name was Flip-Flap Jack.
And he danced upon a table, a table, a table. He danced upon a table.
His name was Flip-Flap Jack.
His mouth was a sausage. A sausage?
 (shrug shoulders and look questioningly)
A sausage!
 (place sausage in mouth position)
His mouth was a sausage. His name was Flip-Flap Jack.
His ears were made of oranges. Oranges?
 (shrug shoulders and look questioningly)
Oranges!
 (place oranges at each side of pancake)
His ears were made of oranges. His name was Flip-Flap Jack.

And he danced upon a table, a table, a table. He danced upon a table.
His name was Flip-Flap Jack.
His body was a golden waffle. A waffle?
    (*shrug shoulders and look questioningly*)
A waffle!
    (*place waffle under pancake touching bottom edge*)
His body was a golden waffle. His name was Flip-Flap Jack.
His arms were two bananas. Bananas?
    (*shrug shoulders and look questioningly*)
Bananas!
    (*place bananas, one on each side of waffle*)
His arms were two bananas. His name was Flip-Flap Jack.
And he danced upon a table, a table, a table. He danced upon a table.
His name was Flip-Flap Jack.
His legs were strips of bacon. Bacon?
    (*shrug shoulders and look questioningly*)
Bacon!
    (*place bacon strips at bottom edge of waffle in leg positions*)
His legs were strips of bacon. His name was Flip-Flap Jack.
His feet were made of french toast. French toast?
    (*shrug shoulders and look questioningly*)
French toast!
(*place french toast one at bottom edge of each strip of bacon*)
His feet were made of french toast. His name was Flip-Flap Jack.
And he danced upon a table, a table, a table. He danced upon a table.
His name was Flip-Flap Jack.
His belly button was a raspberry. A raspberry?
    (*shrug shoulders and look questioningly*)
A raspberry!
    (*place raspberry in the center of the waffle*)
His belly button was a raspberry. His name was Flip-Flap Jack.
There was a man made of food. Made of food? Made of food!
There was a man made of food. HIS NAME WAS FLIP-FLAP JACK!

(*optional audience participation—practice the following rhythm: slap hands on thighs, clap hands together, and then snap fingers every time you sing the phrase, "And he danced upon a table, a table, a table. He danced upon a table. His name was Flip-Flap Jack." Encourage the audience to join you, using the practiced rhythm. For an older audience, the rhythm can be changed slightly, by adding a different rhythm each time you hear "Flip-Flap Jack." Do this by slapping hands on thighs, first palms down, then palms up, then palms down again. This is done quickly, palms down for "Flip," palms up for "Flap," and palms down again for "Jack."*)

To make as a flannel story: (see figures 1.29, 1.30, 1.31, 1.32, and 1.33, pages 46 to 50)

To make as a magnetic story: (see figures 1.29, 1.30, 1.31, 1.32, and 1.33, pages 46 to 50)

FLIP-FLAP-JACK COLORING SHEET

(see figure 1.34, page 51)

PET FOOD ACTIVITY SHEET

(see figures 1.35, 1.36, and 1.37, pages 52 to 54)

"Yum Yum" Support Materials

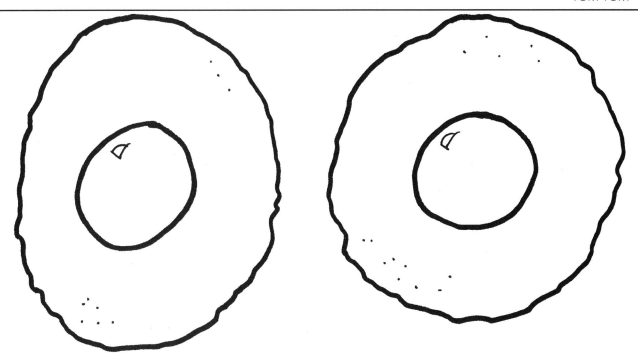

To Make as a Flannel Story

1. Use photocopier to enlarge patterns as you like.
2. Cut all patterns from felt in colors of your choice.
3. Enhance with felt markers.
4. Place on board as indicated in story.
5. Purchase or bring from home an empty egg carton.
6. Optional: encourage audience to join you in singing, "Give it a whack, hear it crack, drop it in the middle, one egg's fryin' on the griddle" to the tune of "This Old Man."

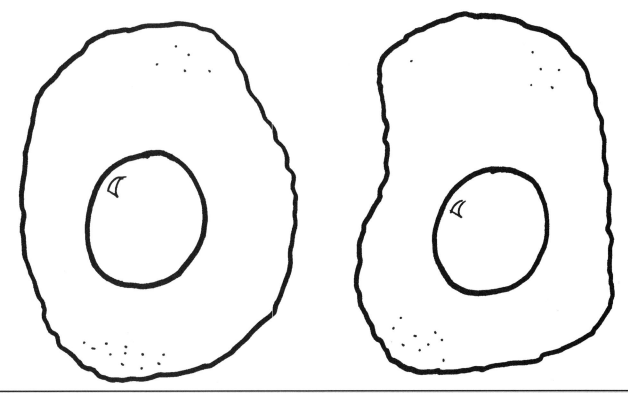

Figure 1.1 Patterns for "Eggs for Breakfast"

Frog Puppet

Materials needed:

- three pieces of green felt; one-half piece of dark green felt
- one-fourth piece of pink felt
- two, two-inch green pompoms
- two, one-inch "googly" eyes
- one 5" x 7" piece of card stock (any color)
- needle and green thread
- one toilet paper roll
- white glue
- scissors

To assemble: (*see figures 1.2, 1.3, 1.4, and 1.5, page 15 to 18*)

Enlarge all patterns on photocopier by 115% or more to best suit your hand-size.

1. Cut out mouth insert, from card stock, and set aside.
2. Cut out all pattern pieces, in felt colors as marked, and set aside.
3. Fold mouth piece in half and place on top of large body piece marked "A" (matching A ends).
4. Sew the mouth to the body, stopping at the fold.
5. Place the other body piece, marked "B," on top of the other side of the mouth piece (matching B ends).
6. Sew the mouth to the body, stopping at the fold.
7. Sew short legs one-half inch from the front of the puppet, marked "X."
8. Sew long legs one inch from back of the puppet, marked "XXX" and finish side seams.
9. Glue dark green spots randomly to legs and back.
10. Place glue inside each end of toilet paper roll and on half (lengthwise) of the outside of the roll.
11. Insert into mouth area "A," glue side down, and tuck felt (frog's "cheeks") into each end of the toilet paper roll forming a dimpled look.
12. Place glue on the top side of the card stock and insert into the mouth section "B," glue side up.
13. Glue tongue into mouth at "C."
14. Sew green pompoms to the top of head, marked "xx."
15. Glue "googly" eyes to the front of each pompom.
16. Glue nose holes into place.
17. When inserting your hand into the frog puppet, your fingers will be on the top side of the toilet paper roll and your thumb under the card stock insert.

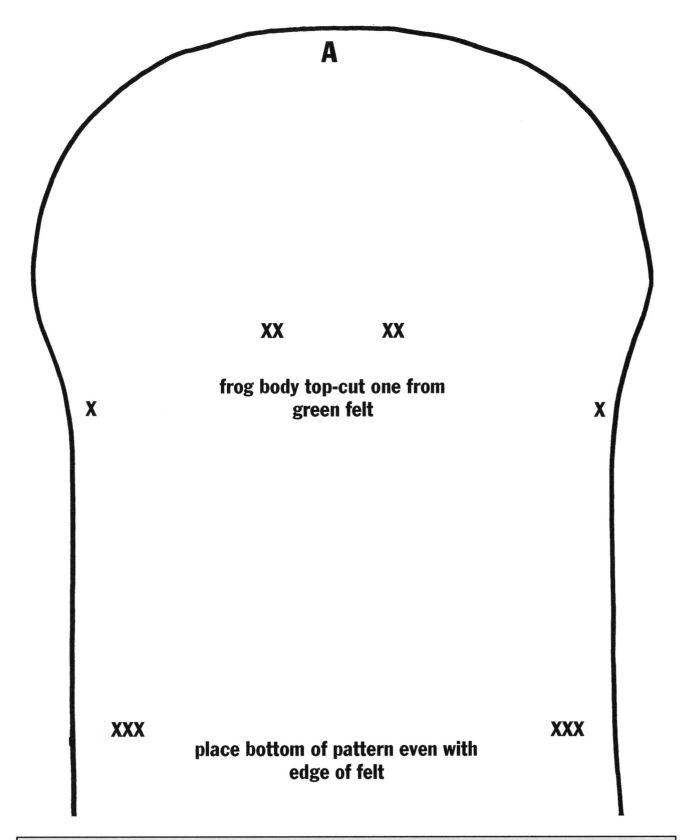

A

XX   XX

frog body top-cut one from
green felt

X   X

XXX   XXX

place bottom of pattern even with
edge of felt

Figure 1.2 Pattern for Frog Puppet

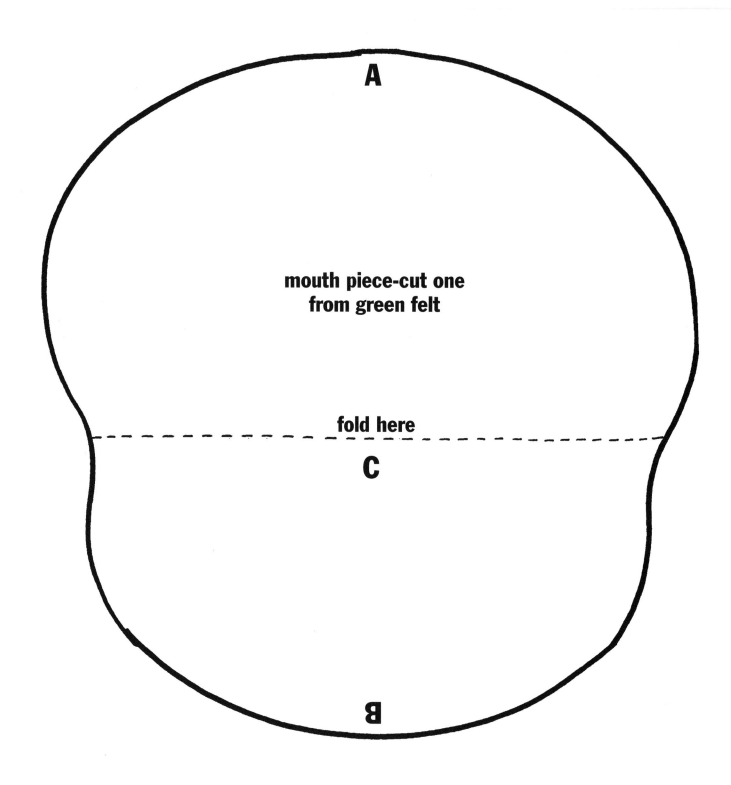

Figure 1.3 Pattern for Frog Puppet

frog body bottom-cut one
from green felt

place bottom of pattern even with
edge of felt

Figure 1.4 Pattern for Frog Puppet

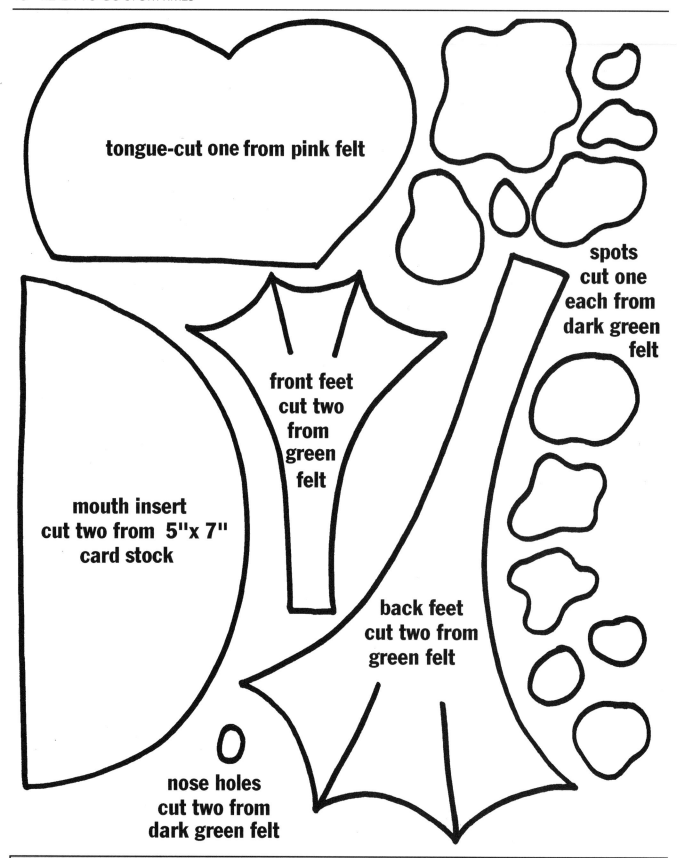

tongue-cut one from pink felt

spots cut one each from dark green felt

front feet cut two from green felt

mouth insert cut two from 5"x 7" card stock

back feet cut two from green felt

nose holes cut two from dark green felt

Figure 1.5 Pattern Pieces for Frog Puppet

Hen Puppet

Materials needed:

- two and one-half pieces of rust-brown felt
- one-half piece goldenrod felt
- one-half piece of red felt
- one-fourth piece yellow felt
- one-eighth piece pink felt
- scrap of black felt
- two, one-half inch "googly" eyes
- one 5"x7" piece of card stock (any color)
- one toilet paper roll needle and rust-brown thread
- stapler
- scissors

To assemble: (see figures 1.6, 1.7, 1.8, 1.9, and 1.10, pages 20 to 24)

Enlarge all patterns on photocopier by 115% or more to best suit your hand-size.

1. Cut out mouth insert, from card stock, and set aside.
2. Cut out all pattern pieces, in colors as marked, and set aside.
3. Fold mouth piece in half and place on top of body piece marked "A" (matching A ends).
4. Sew the mouth to the body, stopping at the fold.
5. Place the other body piece, marked "B," on top of the other side of the mouth piece (matching B ends).
6. Sew the mouth to the body, stopping at the fold.
7. Sew legs one inch from the front of the puppet, marked "X."
8. Place wings right behind the legs, marked "XXX," and finish side seams.
9. Glue nose holes on beak, then glue beak to end of mouth (leaving one and one-half inch hanging over the end of mouth).
10. Glue two eye patches to the top of head, marked "xx."
11. Glue "googly" eyes on top of the eye patch.
12. Sew comb to top of head, marked by "T."
13. Sew wattle under chin, marked by "W."
14. Cut two inches off end of toilet paper roll and discard.
15. Staple one end of remaining toilet paper roll piece closed.
16. Place glue over entire roll and insert into the end of beak area A, with stapled end first.
17. Place glue on the top side of the card stock and insert into mouth section B, glue side up.
18. Glue tongue into mouth at "C."
19. When inserting your hand into the hen puppet, three of your fingers will be in the toilet paper roll; your thumb will be under the card stock insert, in the bottom portion of the hen's mouth.

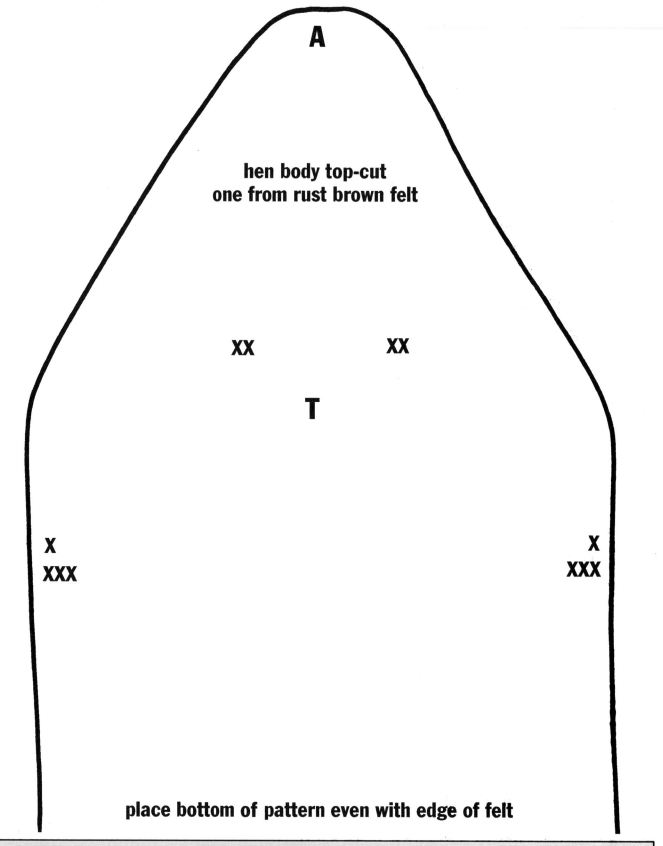

A

**hen body top-cut
one from rust brown felt**

XX   **XX**

T

X
XXX

X
XXX

place bottom of pattern even with edge of felt

Figure 1.6 Pattern for Hen Puppet

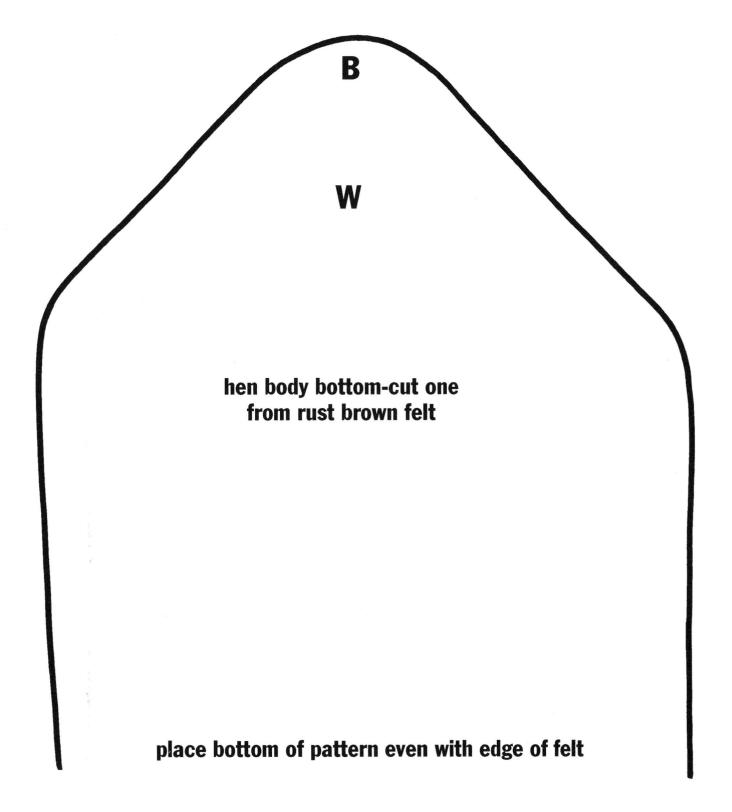

Figure 1.7 Pattern for Hen Puppet

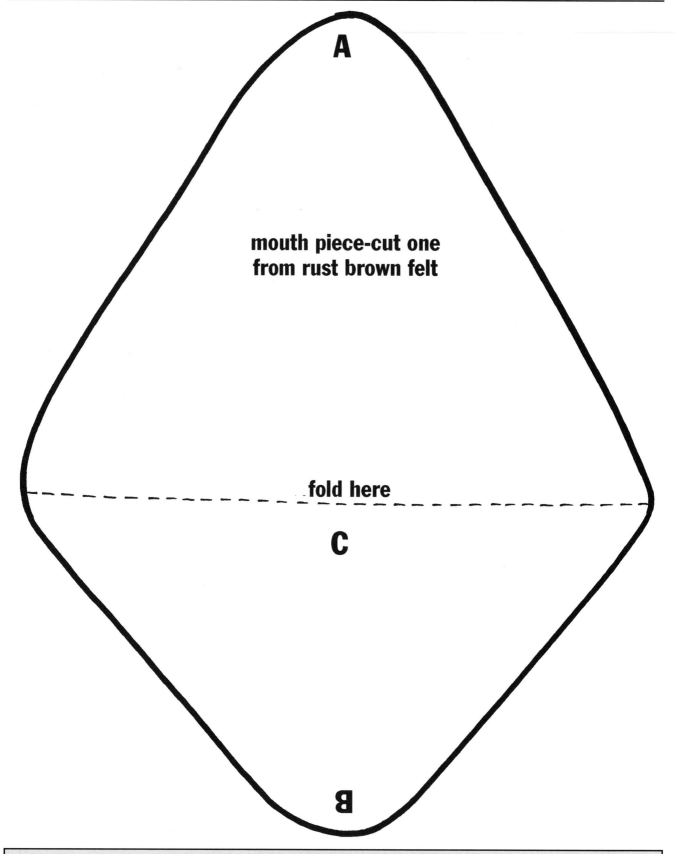

A

**mouth piece-cut one
from rust brown felt**

fold here

C

B

Figure 1.8 Pattern for Hen Puppet

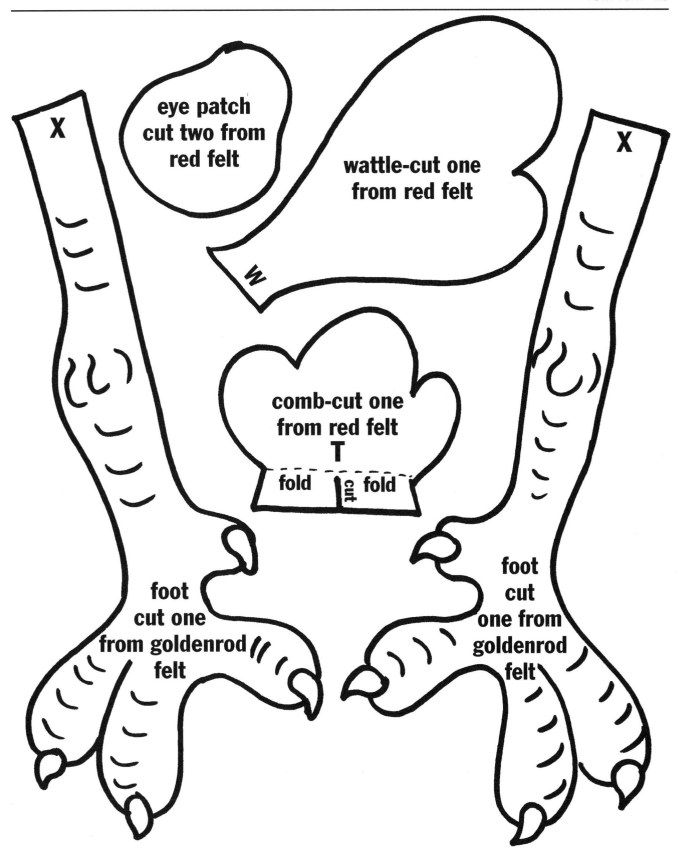

eye patch
cut two from
red felt

wattle-cut one
from red felt

W

X

X

comb-cut one
from red felt
T
fold — cut — fold

foot
cut one
from goldenrod
felt

foot
cut
one from
goldenrod
felt

Figure 1.9 Pattern Pieces for Hen Puppet

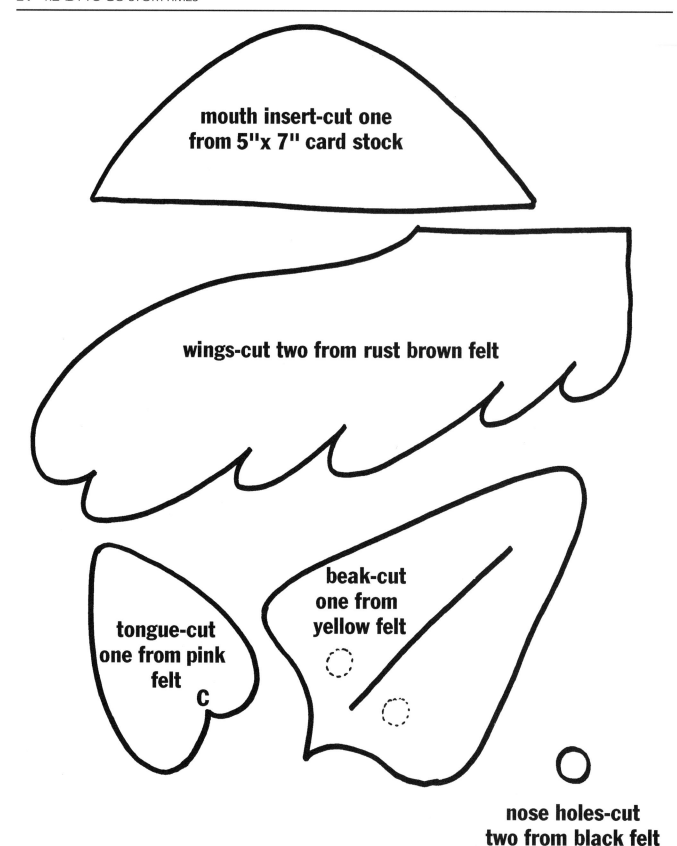

mouth insert-cut one
from 5"x 7" card stock

wings-cut two from rust brown felt

tongue-cut
one from pink
felt
c

beak-cut
one from
yellow felt

nose holes-cut
two from black felt

Figure 1.10 Pattern Pieces for Hen Puppet

Snake Puppet

Materials needed:

- three pieces of black felt
- one piece of red felt
- one piece of yellow felt
- one toilet paper roll
- one 5"x7" piece of card stock (any color)
- six, one-half inch black pompoms
- white glue
- needle and black thread
- stapler
- scissors

To assemble: (*see figures 1.11, 1.12, and 1.13, pages 26 to 28*)

Enlarge all patterns on photocopier by 115% or more to best suit your hand-size.

1. Cut out mouth insert, from card stock, and set aside.
2. Cut out all pattern pieces, in colors as marked, and set aside.
3. Fold mouth piece in half and place on top of body piece marked "A" (matching A ends).
4. Sew the mouth to the body, stopping at the fold.
5. Place the other body piece on top of mouth piece, marked "B" (matching B ends).
6. Sew the mouth to the body, stopping at the fold.
7. Sew stripes to main body (top and bottom) marked "Y" for yellow, "R" for red, and "BB" for black (color order—yellow, red, yellow, black) and finish side seams.
8. Glue three pompoms together forming a pyramid.
9. Glue eyes to front of pompom pyramid.
10. Glue completed eyes in place, marked "xx."
11. Cut two inches off end of toilet paper roll and discard; staple closed one end of remaining half.
12. Place glue over entire roll and insert into mouth section "A," with stapled end first.
13. Place glue on the top side of the card stock and insert into mouth section "B," glue side up.
14. Glue tongue into mouth.
15. When inserting your hand into the snake puppet, three of your fingers will be in the toilet paper roll; your thumb will be under the card stock insert, in the bottom portion of the snake's mouth.

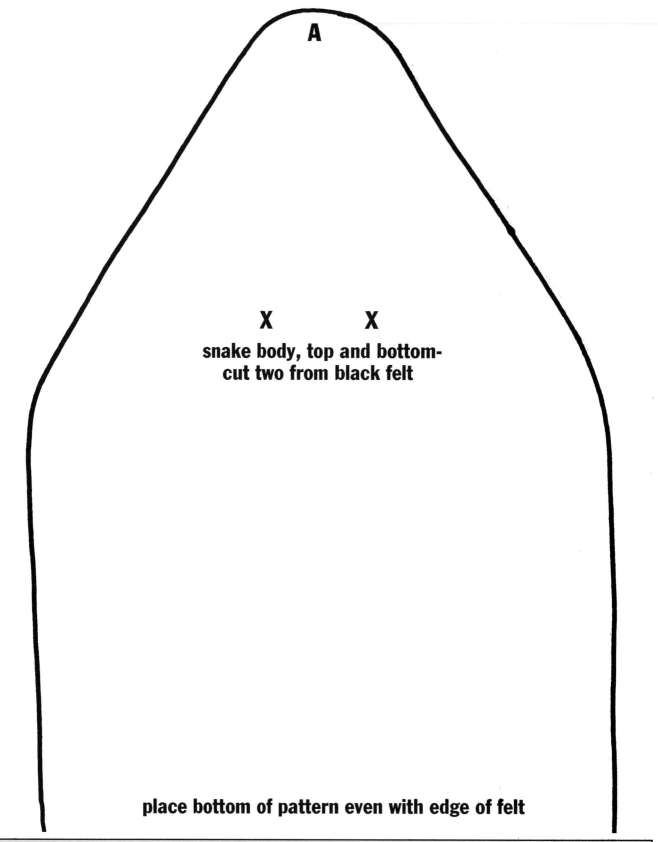

A

X   **X**

**snake body, top and bottom-
cut two from black felt**

place bottom of pattern even with edge of felt

Figure 1.11 Pattern for Snake Puppet

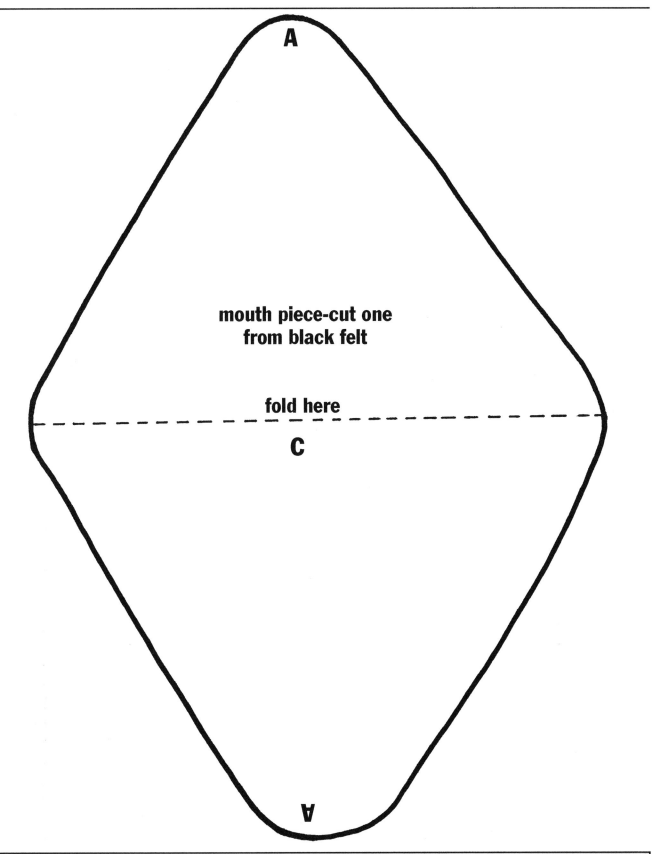

**mouth piece-cut one
from black felt**

fold here

C

A

Figure 1.12 Pattern for Snake Puppet

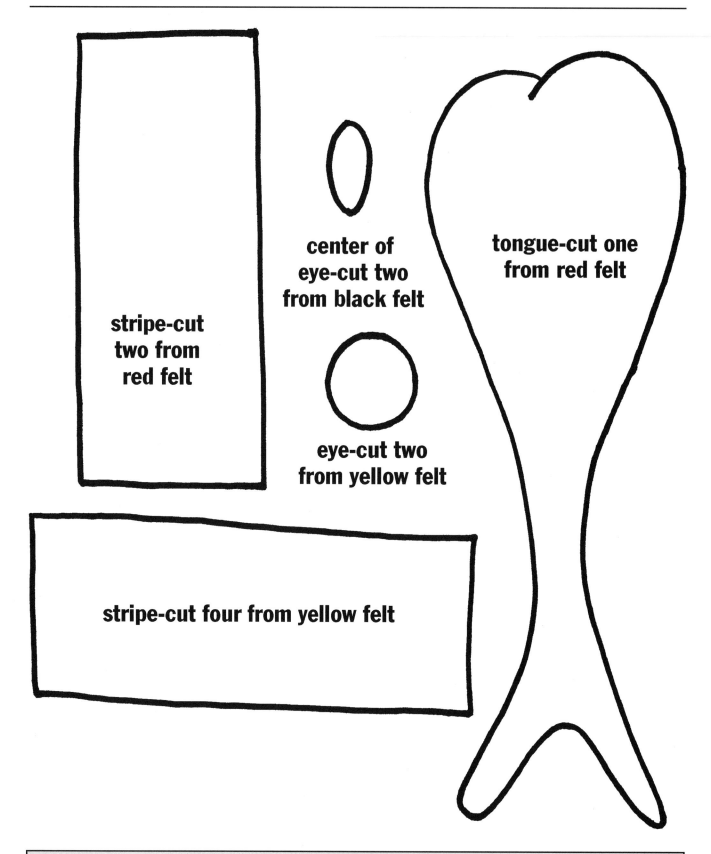

stripe-cut
two from
red felt

center of
eye-cut two
from black felt

tongue-cut one
from red felt

eye-cut two
from yellow felt

stripe-cut four from yellow felt

Figure 1.13 Pattern Pieces for Snake Puppet

Pig Puppet

Materials needed:

- three pieces of pink felt
- one-half piece of black felt
- one-fourth piece of dark pink felt
- one 5"x7" piece of card stock (any color)
- one ten ounce Styrofoam cup
- white glue
- needle and pink thread
- scissors

To assemble: (see figures 1.14, 1.15, and 1.16, pages 30 to 32)

Enlarge all patterns on photocopier by 115% or more to best suit your hand-size.

1. Cut Styrofoam cup in half lengthwise and set aside.
2. Cut out mouth insert, from card stock, and set aside.
3. Cut out all pattern pieces, in colors as marked, and set aside.
4. Sew the round end of the pig snout, marked "A," to the small slightly curved end, marked "A" on the body pattern (matching A ends).
5. Repeat above step for the other body half and snout pieces.
6. Fold mouth piece in half and place on top of body piece marked "A" (matching A ends).
7. Sew the mouth to the body, stopping at the fold.
8. Next place the other body piece, marked "B," on top of the other side of the mouth piece (matching B ends).
9. Sew the mouth to the body, stopping at the fold.
10. Sew two legs one inch from the front of the puppet and two legs one inch from the back of the puppet, marked "X," and finish side seams.
11. Glue hooves on feet.
12. Place glue on one side of the card stock and insert into the bottom of mouth section "A," glue side down.
13. Place glue on the outside of a Styrofoam cup half and glue into the top of mouth section "A," glue side up.
14. Place glue on one side of the other piece of card stock and insert into the top of mouth section "B," glue side up.
15. Place glue on the outside of remaining Styrofoam cup half and glue into the bottom of mouth section "B," glue side down.
16. Fold ear, as marked on pattern, and sew fold.
17. Glue dark pink felt to ear's middle.
18. Sew ears to the top of the puppet's head, marked "D."
19. Glue eyes in place, marked "xx."
20. Glue nose holes in place, marked by "t."

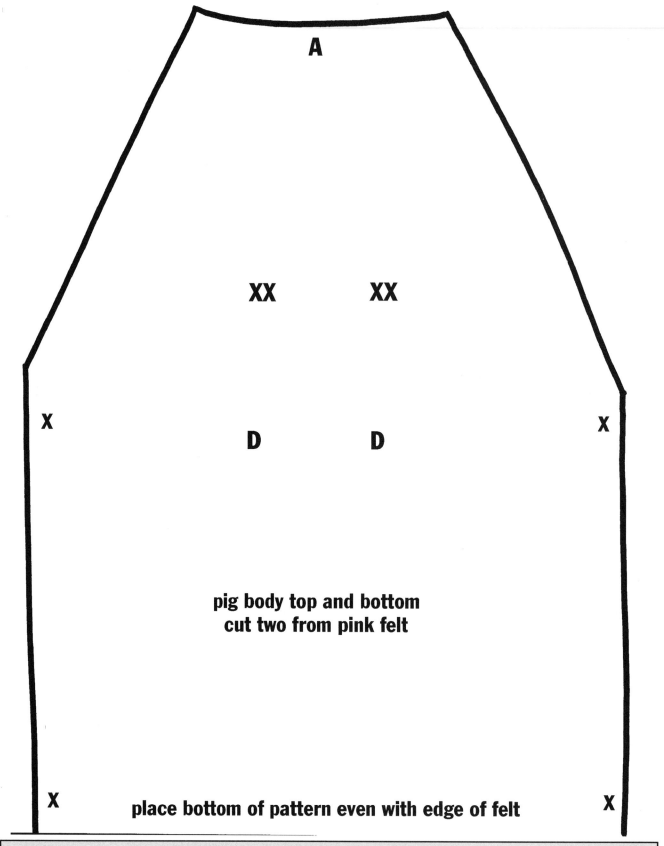

A

XX   XX

X   X

D   D

pig body top and bottom
cut two from pink felt

X   X

place bottom of pattern even with edge of felt

Figure 1.14 Pattern for Pig Puppet

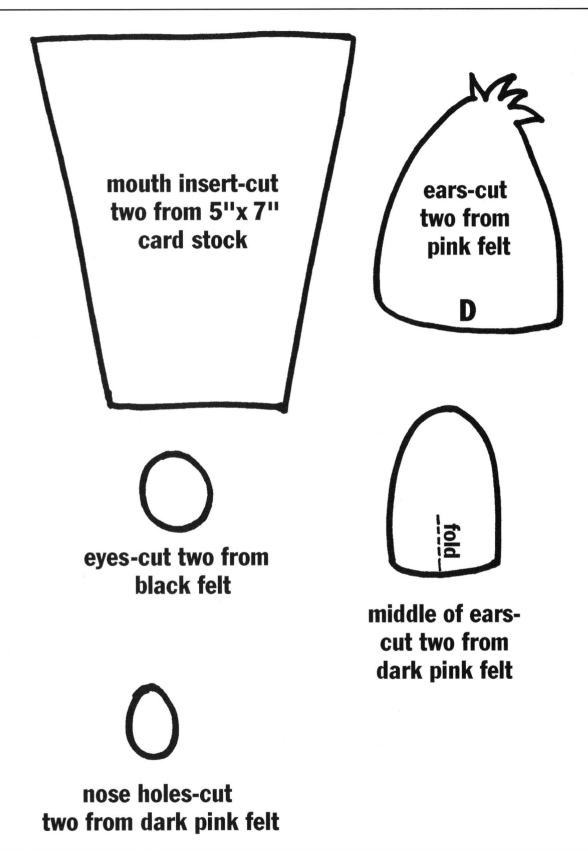

mouth insert-cut
two from 5"x 7"
card stock

ears-cut
two from
pink felt

D

eyes-cut two from
black felt

fold

middle of ears-
cut two from
dark pink felt

nose holes-cut
two from dark pink felt

Figure 1.15 Pattern Pieces for Pig Puppet

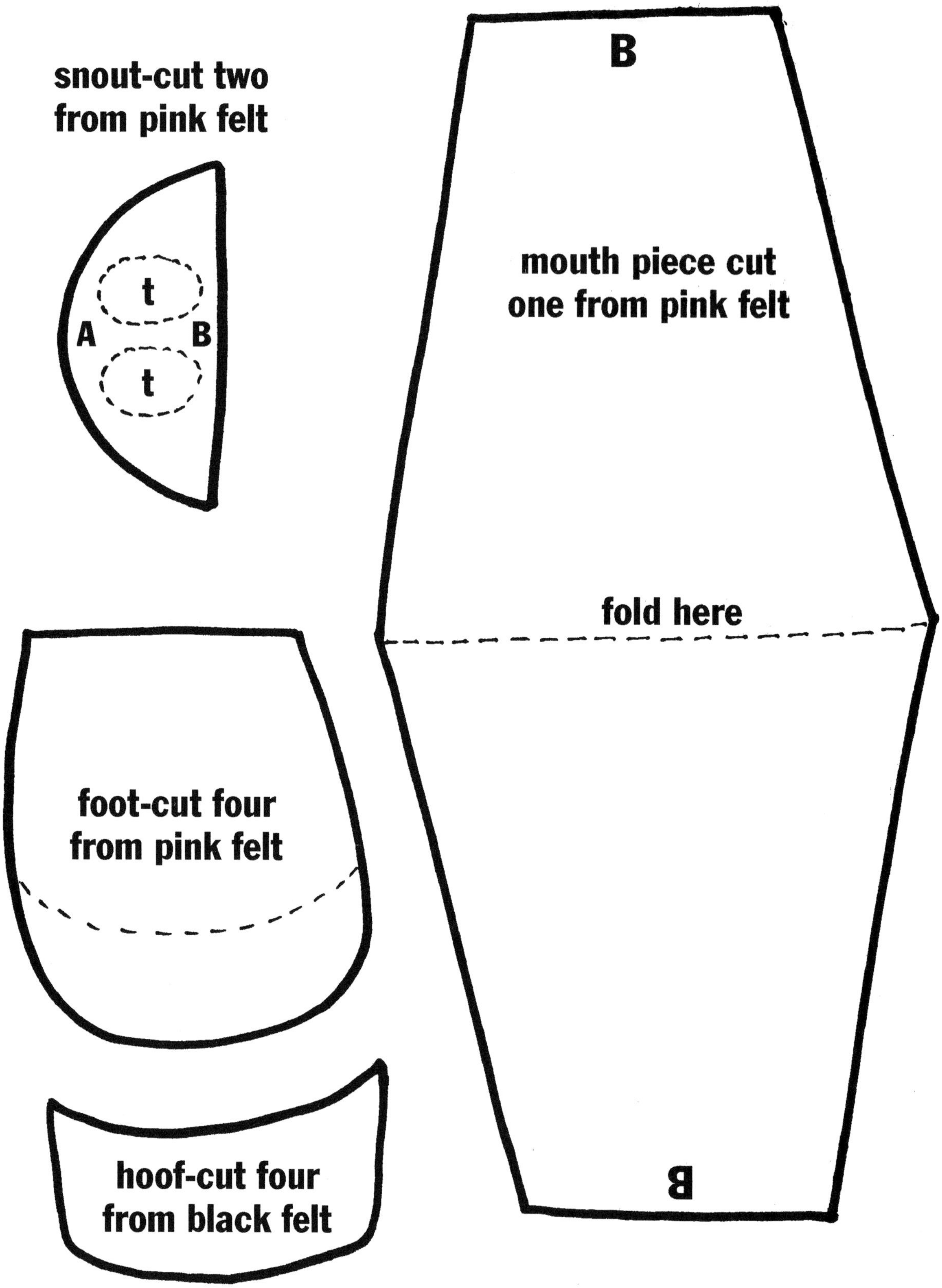

**snout-cut two
from pink felt**

t

t

A   B

**mouth piece cut
one from pink felt**

B

fold here

**foot-cut four
from pink felt**

**hoof-cut four
from black felt**

B

Figure 1.16 Pattern Pieces for Pig Puppet

Rabbit Puppet

Materials needed:

- two and one-half pieces of white felt
- one-half piece of pink felt
- one yard of black embroidery floss
- two, one-half inch black pompoms
- two, one-half inch "googly" eyes
- one 8 1/2"x11" piece of card stock (any color)
- needle and white thread
- small amount of fiber fill or batting
- white glue
- toilet paper roll
- scissors

To assemble: (*see figures 1.17, 1.18, 1.19, and 1.20, pages 34 to 37*)

Enlarge all patterns on photocopier by 115% or more to best suit your hand-size.

1. Cut out mouth inserts, from card stock, and set aside.
2. Cut out all pattern pieces, in colors as marked and set aside.
3. Fold mouth piece in half and place on top of body piece marked "A" (matching A ends).
4. Sew the mouth to the body, stopping at the fold.
5. Place the other body piece, marked "B," on top of the other side of the mouth piece (matching B ends).
6. Sew the mouth to the body, stopping at the fold.
7. Sew feet one inch from the front of puppet, marked "X," and finish side seams.
8. Place glue on one side of card stock and insert into mouth section "A," glue side down.
9. Place glue on one side of remaining card stock and insert into mouth section "B," glue side up.
10. Place a small amount (size of half dollar) of fiber fill into the end of the rabbit's nose, mouth piece "A."
11. Cut one-third off end of toilet paper roll and discard remaining two-thirds roll.
12. Place glue over entire roll and insert firmly against fiber fill in the end of mouth section "A."
13. Place a small amount of fiber fill on either side of toilet paper roll.
14. When inserting your hand into the rabbit puppet, three of your fingers will be in the toilet paper roll; your thumb will be under the card stock insert, in the bottom portion of the rabbit's mouth.
15. Glue tongue into mouth at "C."
16. Glue pink ear pieces, centered on top of white ear pieces, using plenty of glue; let dry.
17. Sew ears to top of puppet's head, marked "D."
18. Press nose in slightly, creating a flat surface to attach nose and teeth.
19. Cut embroidery floss into six, six-inch pieces (whiskers will each be three inches long).
20. Sew in place on both sides of nose; pull ends of floss even; tie a knot to secure.
21. Glue on nose and teeth.
22. Glue pompoms in place, marked "xx."
23. Glue "googly" eyes to front of pompoms.

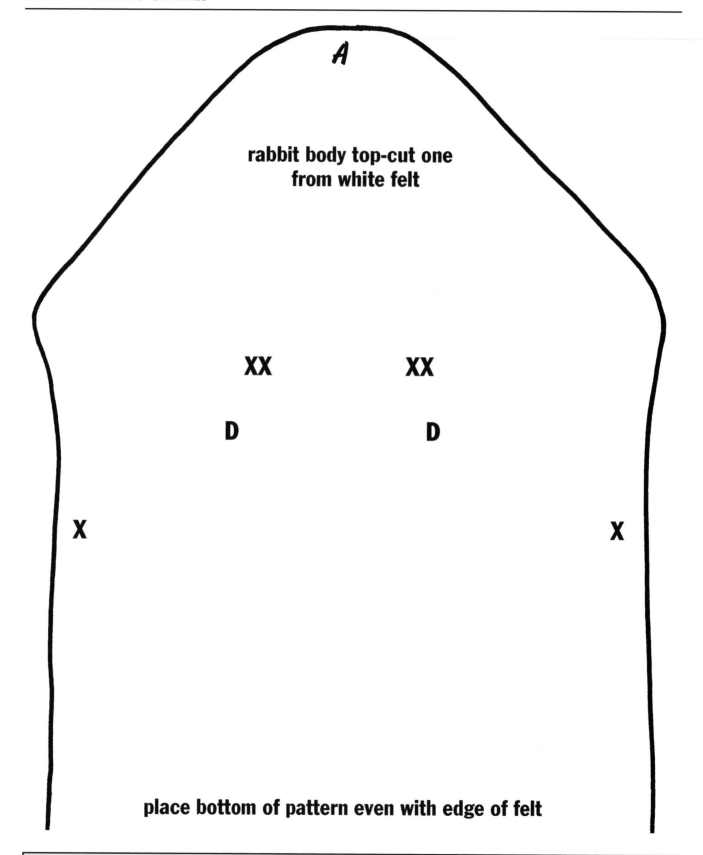

A

**rabbit body top-cut one
from white felt**

XX   **XX**

D   **D**

X   **X**

place bottom of pattern even with edge of felt

Figure 1.17 Pattern for Rabbit Puppet

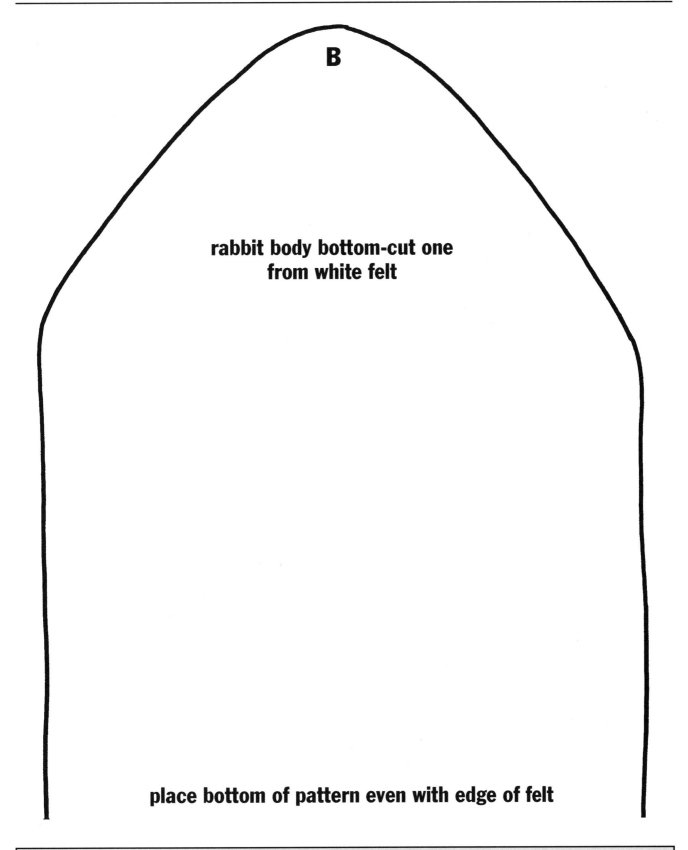

B

rabbit body bottom-cut one
from white felt

place bottom of pattern even with edge of felt

Figure 1.18 Pattern for Rabbit Puppet

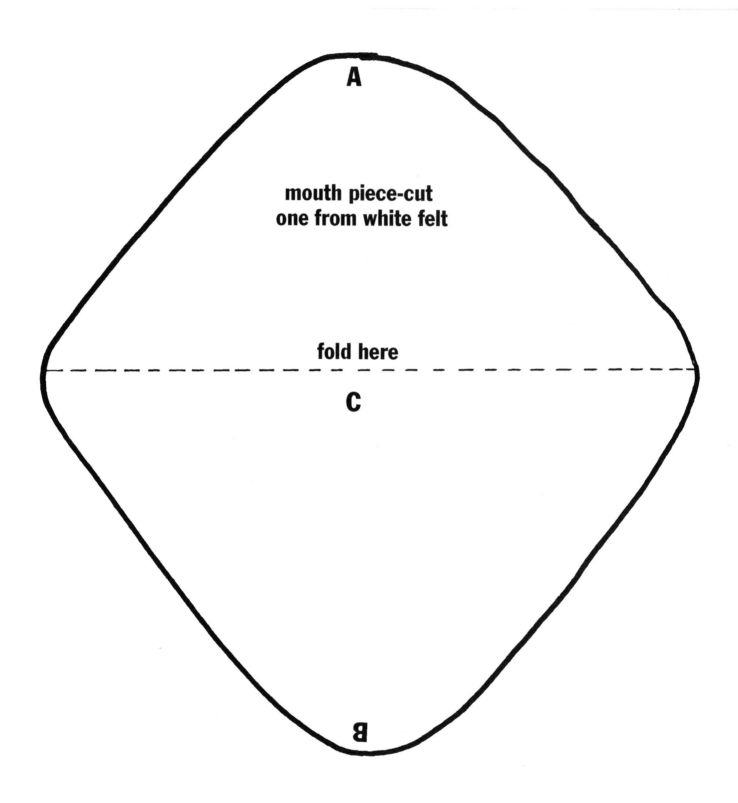

Figure 1.19 Pattern for Rabbit Puppet

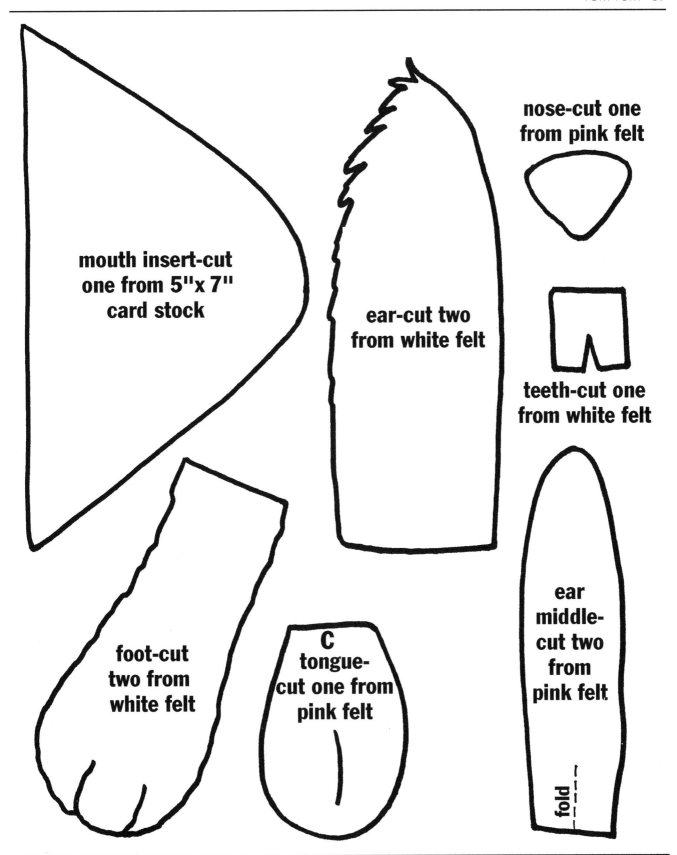

Figure 1.20 Pattern Pieces for Rabbit Puppet

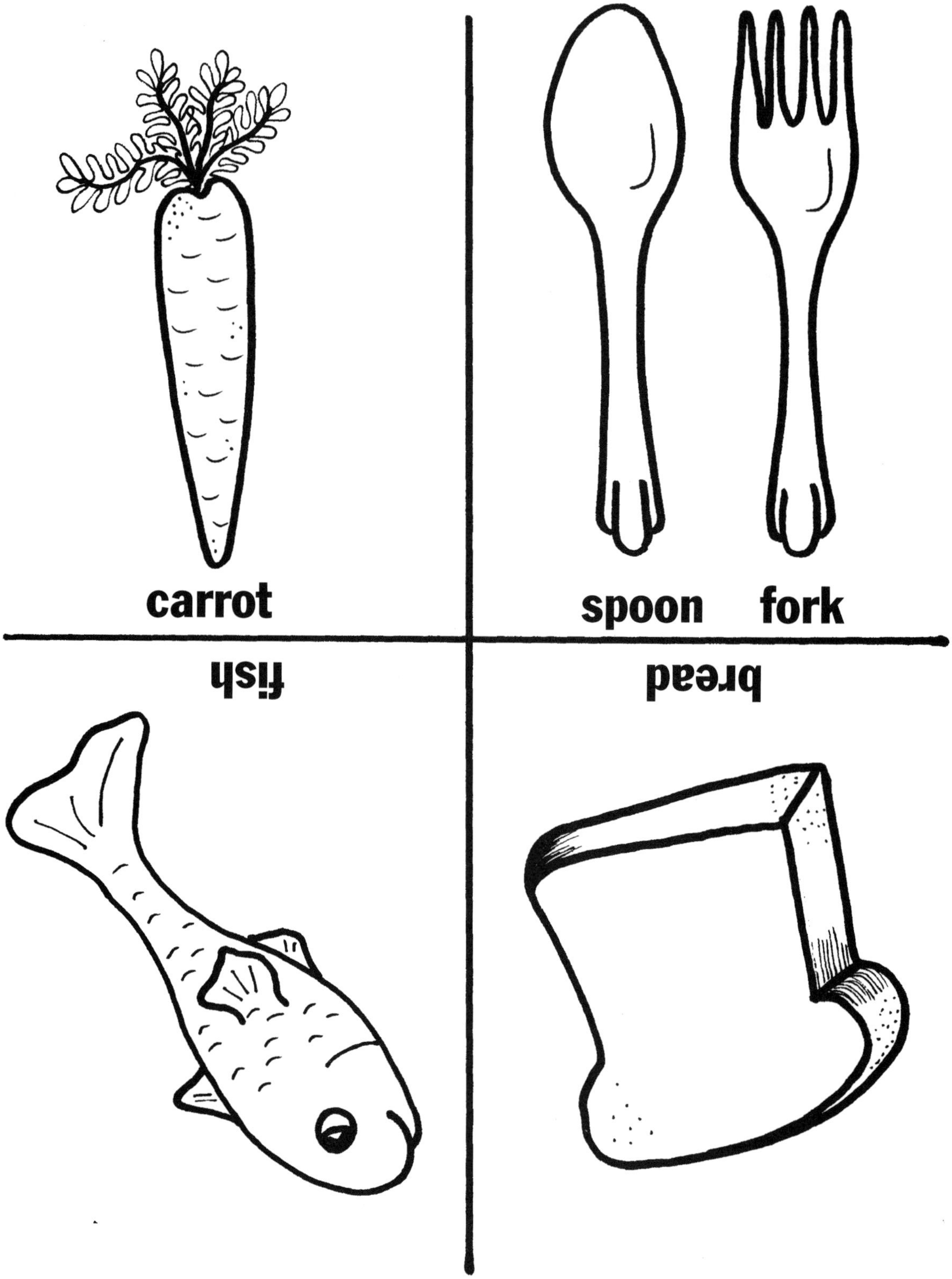

carrot

spoon   fork

fish

bread

Figure 1.21 Cards for Matching Activity

Figure 1.22 Cards for Matching Activity

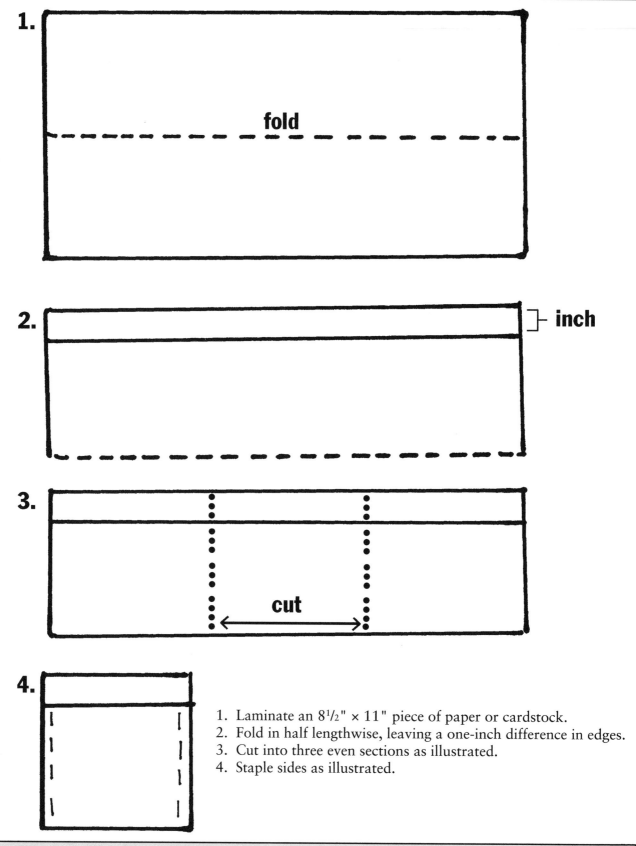

1. Laminate an 8½" × 11" piece of paper or cardstock.
2. Fold in half lengthwise, leaving a one-inch difference in edges.
3. Cut into three even sections as illustrated.
4. Staple sides as illustrated.

Figure 1.23 Pocket to Use with Matching Activity

To Make as a Flannel Story:

1. Enlarge all but Baby Bear pattern by 115%
2. Cut all patterns from felt colors of your choice.
3. Enhance with felt markers.

To Make as a Magnetic Story:

1. Enlarge all but Baby Bear pattern by 115%
2. Color all patterns in colors of your choice.
3. Laminate.
4. Cut out.
5. Attach a magnetic strip to the back of each piece.

Figure 1.24 Mama Bear Pattern for "Bear's Feast"

Figure 1.25 Baby Bear Pattern (smaller than others) for "Bear's Feast"

Figure 1.26 Papa Bear Pattern for "Bear's Feast"

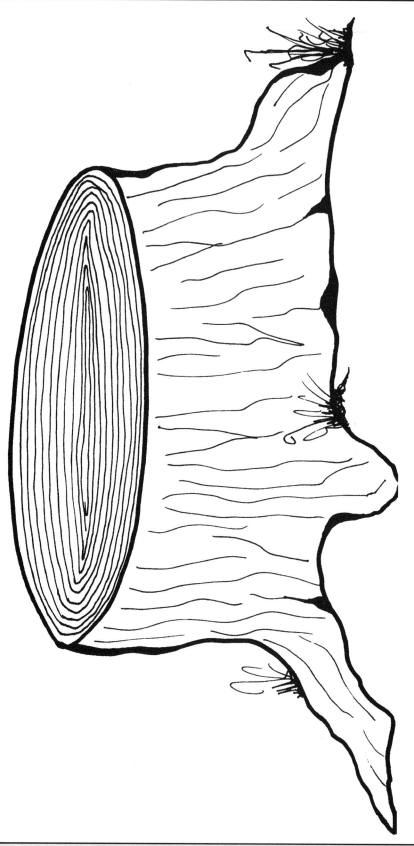

Figure 1.27 Tree Stump Pattern for "Bear's Feast"

Figure 1.28 Apple, Orange, Fish, Acorn, Blueberry Patterns for "Bear's Feast"

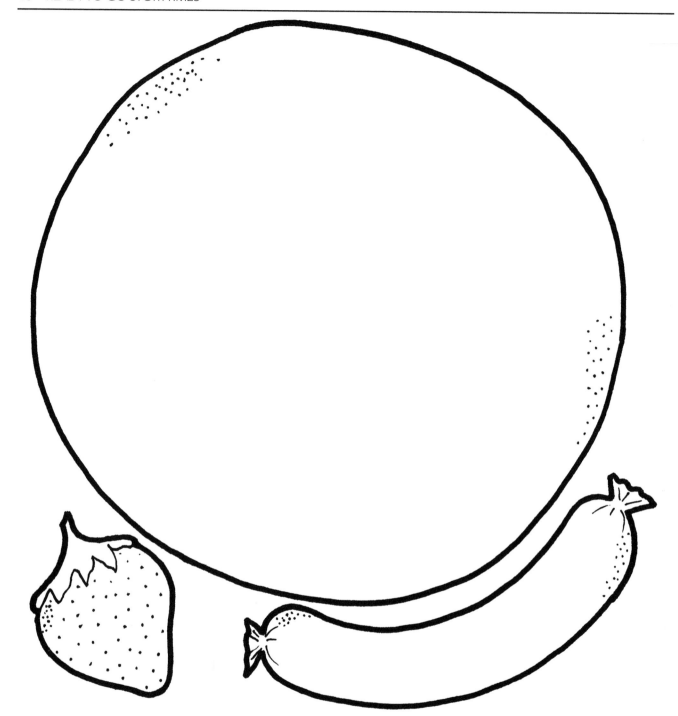

To Make as a Flannel Story:

1. Cut all patterns from felt colors of your choice.
2. Enhance with felt markers.

To Make as a Magnetic Story:

1. Reproduce patterns.
2. Color all patterns in colors of your choice.
3. Laminate.
4. Cut out.
5. Attach a magnetic strip to the back of each piece.

Figure 1.29 Pancake, Strawberry, Sausage Patterns for "Flip-Flap Jack"

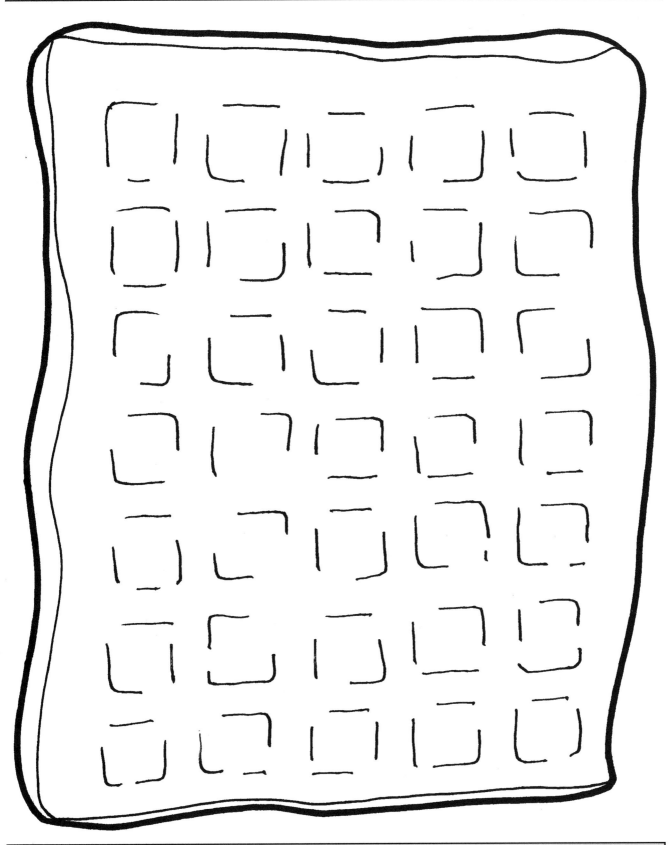

Figure 1.30 Waffle Pattern for "Flip-Flap Jack"

Figure 1.31 FrenchToast, Bacon Patterns for "Flip-Flap Jack"

Figure 1.32 Banana, Raspberry, Blueberry Patterns for "Flip-Flap Jack"

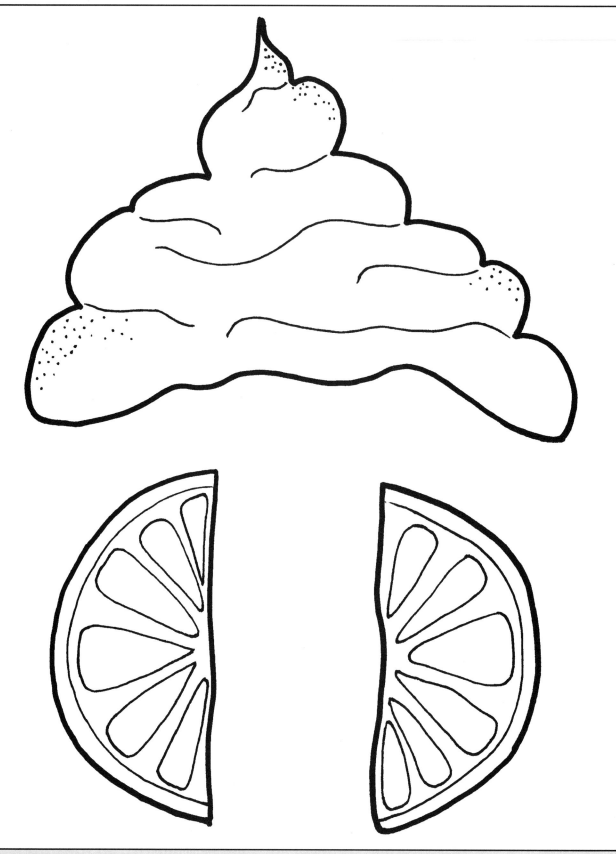

Figure 1.33 Whipped Cream, Orange Slices Patterns for "Flip-Flap Jack"

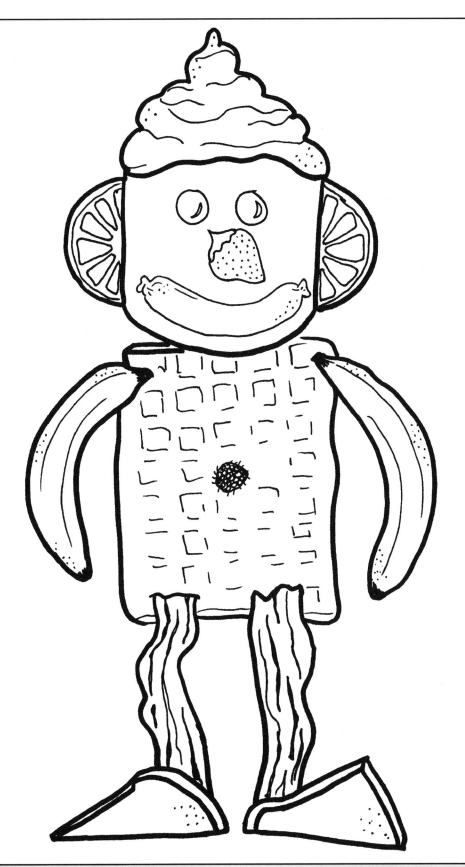

Figure 1.34 Flip-Flap Jack Coloring Sheet

To make matching game:
1. color all pictures and cut apart
2. place all pictures randomly, face up on a flat surface
3. find the pet food for each pet, placing the two cards together
4. continue until all cards are matched

For a variation, you may want to play concentration:
1. spread all cards face down on a flat surface
2. on each turn flip two cards over, revealing both cards: if they match, keep them, if they don't, flip them back over

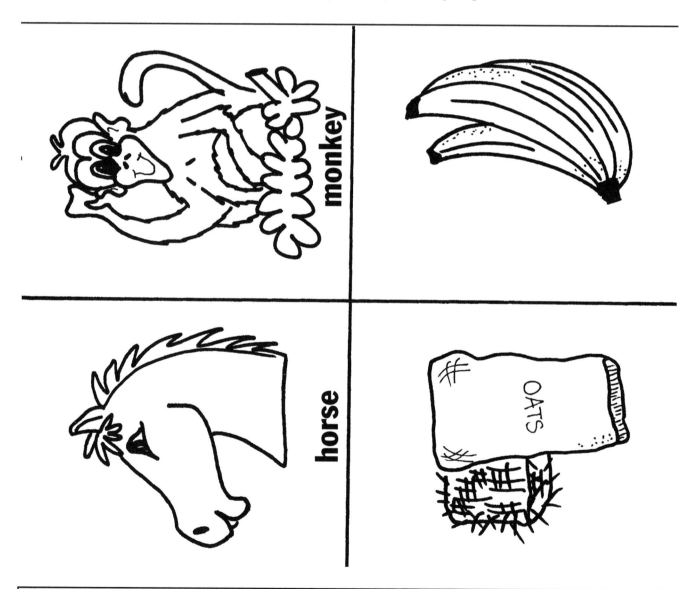

Figure 1.35 Pet Food Matching Activity

Figure 1.36 Pet Food Matching Activity

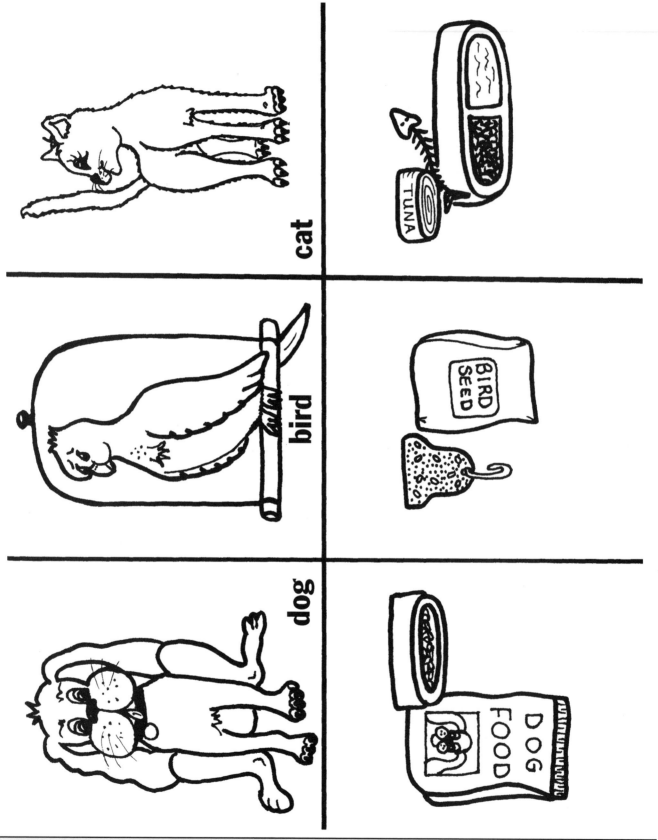

Figure 1.37 Pet Food Matching Activity

CHAPTER TWO

Animal Tales

Animal Tales Outline

Share this safari of animal stories kids will go wild over.

The Welcome Song page 55 (*song #1 from CD*)
Read-A-Loud page 55 (*book*)
We're Gonna Visit the Zoo pages 56 to 57 (*flannel or magnetic story, song #5 from CD*)
One Elephant page 57 (*fingerplay*)
Lou at the Zoo page 58 (*magnetic story*)
Five Bears pages 58 to 59 (*magnetic story*)
Matching page 59 (*parent and child activity*)
The Stretch and Sit Song page 60 (*song #2 from CD*)
Berry Pickin' pages 60 to 61 (*interactive story*)
Let's Go for a Jungle Walk pages 61 to 62 (*action song, song #6 from CD*)
Visit the Zoo Coloring Sheet page 104 (*handout*)
Wild Animal Concentration Activity Sheet pages 105 to 106 (*handout*)

THE WELCOME SONG

(*play song #1 from CD to let children know you are ready to begin*) Let's begin our storytime, see a play, and hear a rhyme. Welcome mom and daddy too, they can sit right next to you. Songs to sing and books to see, you'll have fun each week with me.

READ-A-LOUD

Choose a book related to wild animals, we recommend reading Roar! A Noisy Counting Book *by Pamela Duncan Edwards, illustrated by Henry Cole (New York: Harper Collins Publishers, 2000).*

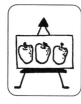

WE'RE GONNA VISIT THE ZOO

(play song #5 from CD)
Today we're gonna visit the big elephants at the zoo,
 (place elephant, wearing trunks, on board)
and our teacher said that we might even learn a thing or two.
 (chastise with finger, hold up one finger, then hold up two fingers)
When summer days get hotter,
 (use hand to fan flannel elephant)
elephants wade right in the water
 (walk in place)
and they don't even wear any trunks. No trunks!?
 (remove elephant's swim trunks)
Today we're gonna visit kangaroos at the zoo,
 (place kangaroo, wearing boxing gloves, on board)
and our teacher said that we might even learn a thing or two.
 (chastise with finger, hold up one finger, then hold up two fingers)
With a babe in their pocket,
 (pretend to rock baby, then using both hands, point to your pre-
 tend kangaroo pocket)
when they box they really sock it.
 (then make boxing motion with fists)
and they don't even wear a glove. No glove!?
 (remove boxing gloves from kangaroo)
Today we're gonna visit the green parrots at the zoo,
 (place parrot, holding pencil on board)
and our teacher said that we might even learn a thing or two.
 (chastise with finger, hold up one finger, then hold up two fingers)
It seems they're always squawking,
 (use hand to make talking motion)
but like us they're only talking
 (point to self)
and they don't even go to school. No school!?
 (remove pencil)
Today we're gonna visit the wild ostrich at the zoo,
 (place ostrich, wearing tennis shoes, on board)
and our teacher said that we might even learn a thing or two.
 (chastise with finger, hold up one finger, then hold up two fingers)
When they fly it doesn't last,
 (flap arms to resemble a bird's wings)
that's why they run really fast.
 (run in place)
and they don't even wear tennis shoes. No shoes!?
 (remove tennis shoes)

Today while we were visiting the animals at the zoo, we listened to our teacher
> (*cup hand behind ear*)

and we learned a thing or two.
> (*chastise with finger, hold up one finger, then hold up two fingers*)

It sure was lots of fun naming each and every one,
> (*using right hand, point to each finger of the left hand*)

and we didn't even take a test. No test!?
> (*hold up slate*)

To make as a flannel story: (see figures 2.1, 2.2, 2.3, 2.4, 2.5, and 2.6, pages 65 to 70)

To make slate: (see figure 2.6, page 70)

To make as a magnetic story: (see figures 2.1, 2.2, 2.3, 2.4, 2.5, and 2.6, pages 65 to 70)

ONE ELEPHANT

The zoo has one elephant.
> (*place arm in front of face to resemble an elephant's trunk, then make trumpeting sound every time you say the word elephant*)

The zoo has two lions,
> (*hold up hands to resemble lion's paws, then make roaring sound every time you say the word lions*)

and one elephant.
The zoo has three zebras,
> (*prance in place, then make braying sound every time you say the word zebras*)

two lions, and one elephant.
The zoo has four flamingos,
> (*stand on one leg, then make fluting sound every time you say the word flamingos*)

three zebras, two lions, and one elephant.
The zoo has five monkeys,
> (*hold one hand in the air and scratch arm pit, then make monkey noise every time you say the word monkeys*)

four flamingos, three zebras, two lions,
> (*pause and say slowly with emphasis*)

and one elephant.

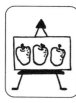

LOU AT THE ZOO

(before beginning, put all animals behind their habitats and place on board in the following order: monkey, elephant, giraffe, polar bear, and snake)

My name is Lou, I work at the zoo. Feeding the animals, can you guess who?

(point to first picture, then give the children a few hints, for example, "He lives in the trees and eats bananas"—reveal the monkey after the children guess)

My name is Lou, I work at the zoo. Feeding the animals, can you guess who?

(point to second picture, then give the children a few hints, for example, "He has BIG ears and he eats hay"—reveal the elephant after the children guess)

My name is Lou, I work at the zoo. Feeding the animals, can you guess who?

(point to third picture, then give the children a few hints, for example, "He has a long neck and eats leaves"—reveal the giraffe after the children guess)

My name is Lou, I work at the zoo. Feeding the animals, can you guess who?

(point to fourth picture, then give the children a few hints, for example, "He is white and eats seals and fish"—reveal the polar bear after the children guess)

My name is Lou, I work at the zoo. Feeding the animals, can you guess who?

(point to fifth picture, then give the children a few hints, for example, "He hisses and eats mice"—reveal the snake after the children guess)

My name is Lou, I'm through at the zoo. Now I'm going to sleep for an hour or two.

(rest head on hands as if sleeping and snore)

To make as a magnetic story: (see figures 2.7, 2.8, 2.9, 2.10, 2.11, 2.12, 2.13, 2.14, 2.15, and 2.16, pages 71 to 80)

FIVE BEAR CUBS

Said the first bear cub as he scratched at fleas,
　　(place one bear cub on board)
"Oh I wish I had a hive of honey bees."
　　(place bee hive on board next to bear one)
Said the second bear cub, as he sniffed about,

(*place second bear cub on board*)
"Oh I wish I had a nice big trout."
　　(*place trout on board next to bear two*)
Said the third bear cub, as he began to scratch,
　　(*place third bear cub on board*)
"Oh I wish I was in a strawberry patch."
　　(*place strawberries on board next to bear three*)
Said the fourth bear cub, as he rolled on the ground,
　　(*place fourth bear cub on board*)
"Oh I wish I had some bugs all around."
　　(*place bugs on board next to bear four*)
Said the fifth bear cub, as he gave a wink,
　　(*place fifth bear cub on board*)
"Oh I wish I had some water to drink."
　　(*place water puddle on board next to bear five*)
Said the sleepy mother bears, "We don't need a thing, 'cause we're big and fat and were sleepin' 'til spring."
　　(*make snoring sound*)

To make as a magnetic board: (see figures 2.17, 2.18, 2.19, 2.20, 2.21, 2.22, and 2.23, pages 81 to 87)

MATCHING

A packet, consisting of a three-section pocket, each with a picture secured to the front, and nine loose picture cards, is given to each child. The child and parent work together, placing loose picture cards into the appropriate pocket. Make one packet for every child. Pictures may be stored in the middle section of the three-section pocket.

To make picture cards: (see figures 2.24, 2.25, and 2.26, pages 88 to 90)

To make a three-section pocket: (see figures 2.27 and 2.28, pages 91 to 92)

To introduce the activity, hold up the zebra card and ask the children a sample question. "Does a zebra live in the water?" The response will be no, then ask, "Does a zebra live in the sky?" The response will again be no. Then ask, "Does a zebra live on the land?" When the children answer yes, place the zebra into the land pocket.

THE STRETCH AND SIT SONG

(*play song #2 from CD*)
Let's stand up together. Now let's all touch our nose. Put our hands in the air high, bend down, and touch our toes. Let's stand up together. Now let's all touch our nose. Put our hands in the air high, bend down, and touch our toes. Now it's time to listen so sit right on the floor. Hands are in our laps now and we are ready for more.

BERRY PICKIN'

(*before beginning, divide group into four sections and assign some-one in each section to hold a picture, being sure to keep them in numerical order; let each section practice their noise; the bee sec-tion will make a buzzing sound each time they hear the phrase, "five bees buzzed"; the field mice section will pat hands on thighs each time they hear the phrase, "four field mice ran"; the wolf section will howl each time they hear the phrase, "three wolves howled"; the owl section will hoot each time they hear the phrase, "two owls hooted"; the storyteller plays the part of the little girl*)
(*little girl*)
"I'm hungry, my tummy's growling."
(*rub stomach*)
"I think I'll pick some berries."
(*pretend to pick berries*)
Just then five bees buzzed.
Five bees buzzed, and four field mice ran.
Five bees buzzed, four field mice ran, and three wolves howled.
Five bees buzzed, four field mice ran, three wolves howled, and two owls hooted.
Then five bees buzzed,
(*bees buzz and don't stop*)
four field mice ran,
(*mice run and don't stop*)
three wolves howled,
(*wolves howl and don't stop*)
and two owls hooted.
(*owls hoot and don't stop*)
(*little girl yells loudly*)
"Stop that noise!"
(*pause*)
"And here's the reason, ya gotta be quiet in berry pickin' season."
(*pause until everyone is quiet, then hold stuffed bear and say*)
One big scary bear growled, "Grrrrr!"

(*little girl*)
"Was that your tummy growling? You must be hungry too."
"Do you want to pick berries with me?"
  (*whisper*)
"But remember, you gotta be quiet during berry pickin' season."
  (*walk away from group still holding bear*)

To prepare pictures: (see figures 2.29, 2.30, 2.31, 2.32, and 2.33, pages 93 to 97)

LET'S GO FOR A JUNGLE WALK

(*prior to your storytime hang animal pictures around the room*)
(*see figures 2.34, 2.35, 2.36, 2.37, and 2.38, pages 98 to 102*)
(*have children stand, give each child a pair of paper binoculars,
(see figure 2.39, page 103) play song #6 from CD; have children
follow you in a circle around the room and look for each animal
as it is named in the song*)
Let's go for a jungle walk
  (*beckon with hand*)
and listen to the animals talk,
  (*cup hand behind ear*)
grab your binoculars and we're on our way!
  (*hold binoculars up with both hands*)
Look at the great big crocodile.
  (*look at crocodile picture through binoculars and encourage children to do the same*)
Doesn't he have a beautiful smile?
We could watch him swim all night and day!
Let's go for a jungle walk
  (*beckon with hand*)
and listen to the animals talk,
  (*cup hand behind ear*)
grab your binoculars and we're on our way!
  (*hold binoculars up with both hands*)
There's a monkey in the tree.
  (*look at monkey picture through binoculars and encourage children to do the same*)
Way up high in the canopy.
Doesn't he have an awesome place to play!
Let's go for a jungle walk
  (*beckon with hand*)
and listen to the animals talk,
  (*cup hand behind ear*)

grab your binoculars and we're on our way!
  (*hold binoculars up with both hands*)
Look at the giraffe so tall and proud.
  (*look at giraffe picture through binoculars and encourage children to do the same*)
Looks like he could touch a cloud.
I bet he can see one hundred miles away!
Let's go for a jungle walk
  (*beckon with hand*)
and listen to the animals talk,
  (*cup hand behind ear*)
grab your binoculars and we're on our way!
  (*hold binoculars up with both hands*)
There's a zebra with her foal.
  (*look at zebra picture through binoculars and encourage children to do the same*)
Drinking at the watering hole.
They're getting ready for the long hot day!
Let's go for a jungle walk
  (*beckon with hand*)
and listen to the animals talk,
  (*cup hand behind ear*)
grab your binoculars and we're on our way!
  (*hold binoculars up with both hands*)
Look at the snake hanging from the tree.
  (*look at snake picture through binoculars and encourage children to do the same*)
He's sticking out his tongue at me.
Think I'd better hurry on my way!
We went for a jungle walk
  (*beckon with hand*)
and listened to the animals talk,
  (*cup hand behind ear*)
Wasn't it fun to watch them run and play?
Glad the animals let us spy.
Now it's time to say goodbye.
  (*wave goodbye with hand*)
Let's save our binoculars for another day!

To prepare animal pictures: (see figures 2.34, 2.35, 2.36, 2.37, and 2.38, pages 98 to 102)

To make paper binoculars: (see figure 2.39, page 103)

VISIT THE ZOO COLORING SHEET

(see figure 2.40, page 104)

WILD ANIMAL CONCENTRATION ACTIVITY SHEET

(see figures 2.41 and 2.42, pages 105 and 106)

"Animal Tales" Support Materials

To Make as a Flannel Story:

1. Cut all patterns, except slate, from felt colors of your choice.
2. Enhance with markers.

To Make as a Magnetic Story:

1. Reproduce patterns.
2. Color all patterns in colors of your choice.
3. Laminate.
4. Cut out.
5. Attach a magnetic strip to the back of each piece.

Figure 2.1 Pattern for "We're Gonna Visit the Zoo"

Figure 2.2 Pattern for "We're Gonna Visit the Zoo"

Figure 2.3 Pattern for "We're Gonna Visit the Zoo"

Figure 2.4 Pattern for "We're Gonna Visit the Zoo"

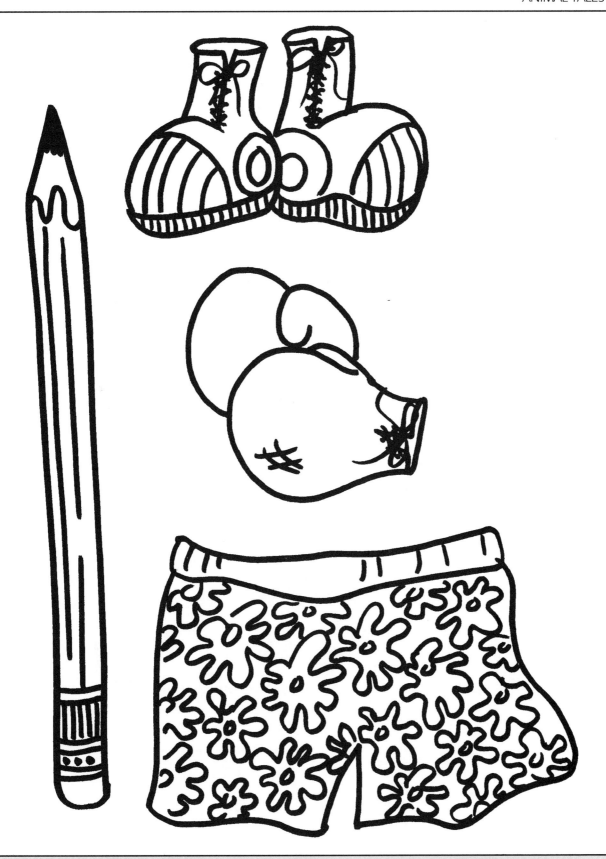

Figure 2.5 Patterns for "We're Gonna Visit the Zoo"

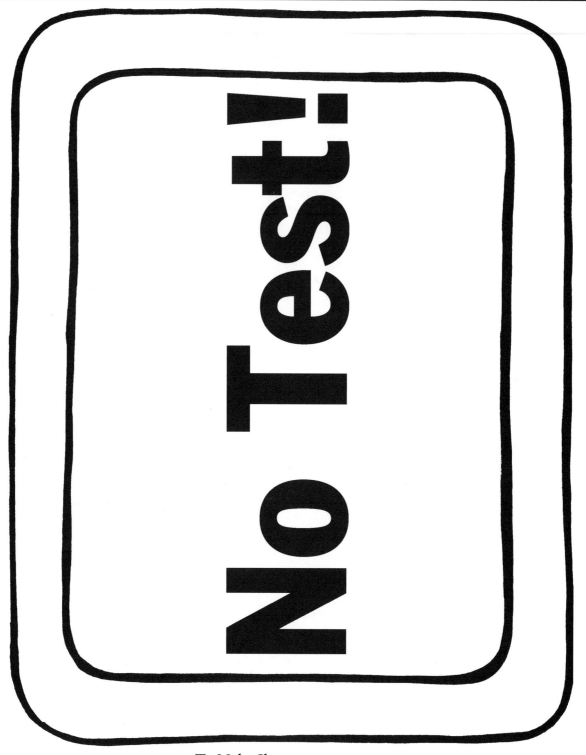

To Make Slate:

1. Color slate pattern in color of your choice.
2. Laminate.
3. Cut out.

Figure 2.6 Pattern for "We're Gonna Visit the Zoo"

To Make as a Magnetic Story:

1. Purchase or bring from home a ring of keys and a safari hat.
2. Reproduce patterns.
3. Color all pictures in colors of your choice.
4. Laminate.
5. Cut out.
6. Attach a magnetic strip to the back of each piece.

Figure 2.7 Pattern for Monkey's Habitat in "Lou at the Zoo"

Figure 2.8 Pattern for Monkey in "Lou at the Zoo"

Figure 2.9 Pattern for Elephant's Habitat in "Lou at the Zoo"

Figure 2.10 Pattern for Elephant in "Lou at the Zoo"

Figure 2.11 Pattern for Giraffe's Habitat in "Lou at the Zoo"

Figure 2.12 Pattern for Giraffe in "Lou at the Zoo"

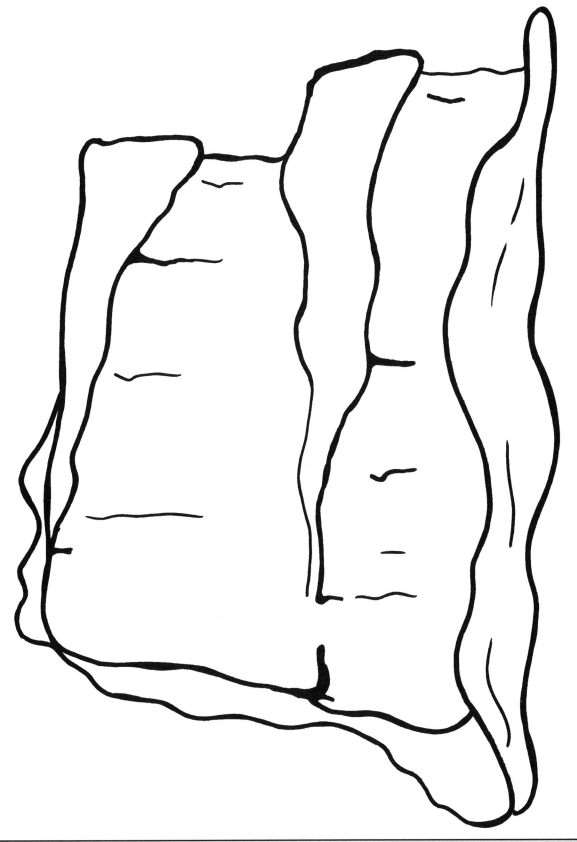

Figure 2.13 Pattern for Polar Bear's Habitat in "Lou at the Zoo"

Figure 2.14 Pattern for Polar Bear in "Lou at the Zoo"

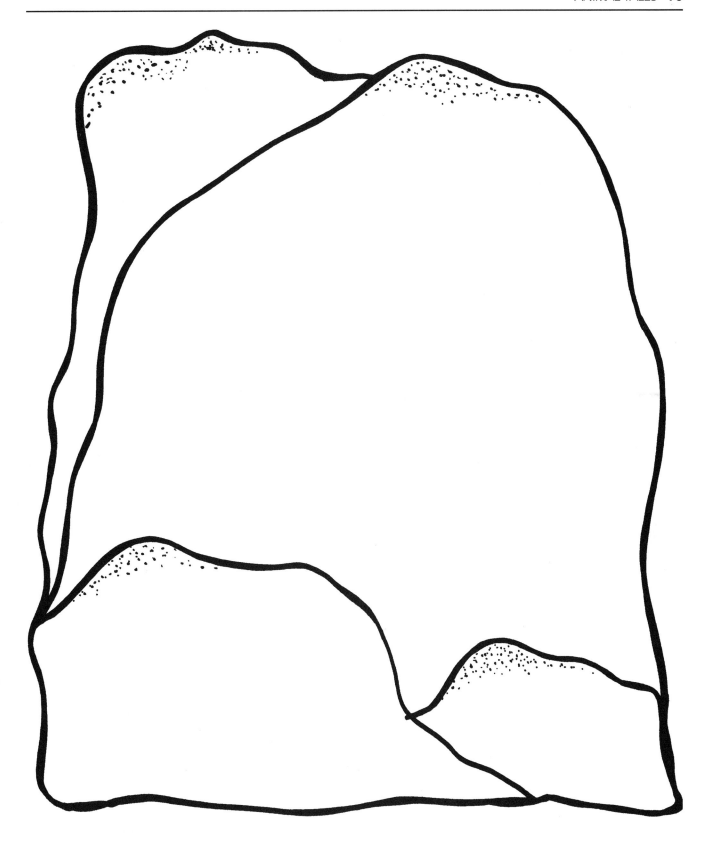

Figure 2.15 Pattern for Snake's Habitat in "Lou at the Zoo"

Figure 2.16 Pattern for Snake in "Lou at the Zoo"

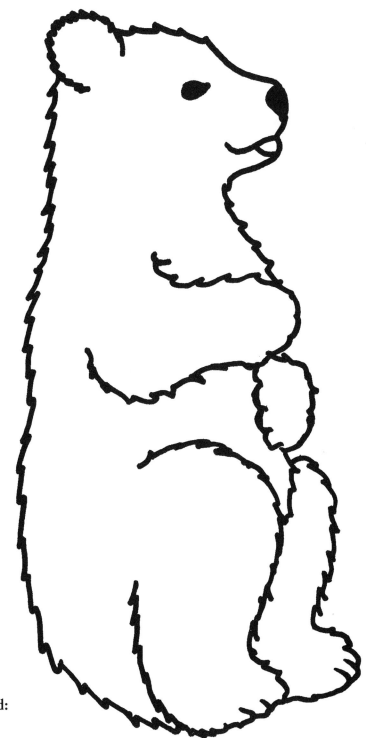

To Make as a Magnetic Board:

1. Reproduce patterns.
2. Color all patterns in colors of your choice.
3. Laminate.
4. Cut out.
5. Attach a magnetic strip to the back of each piece.

Figure 2.17 Pattern for First Bear in "Five Bear Cubs"

Figure 2.18 Pattern for Second Bear in "Five Bear Cubs"

Figure 2.19 Pattern for Third Bear in "Five Bear Cubs"

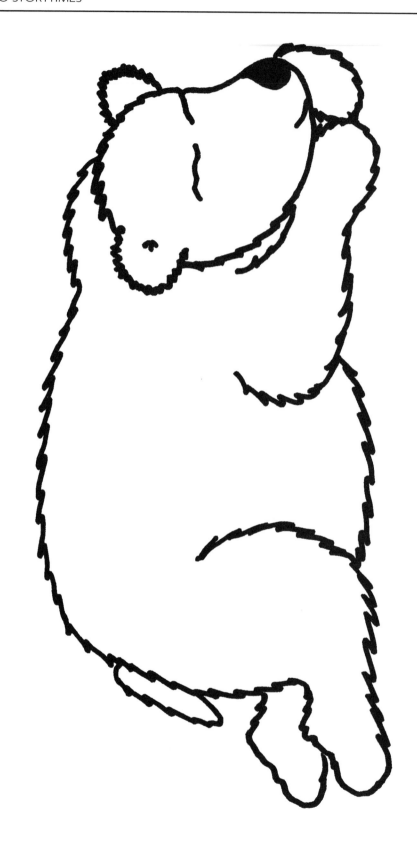

Figure 2.20 Pattern for Fourth Bear in "Five Bear Cubs"

Figure 2.21 Pattern for Fifth Bear in "Five Bear Cubs"

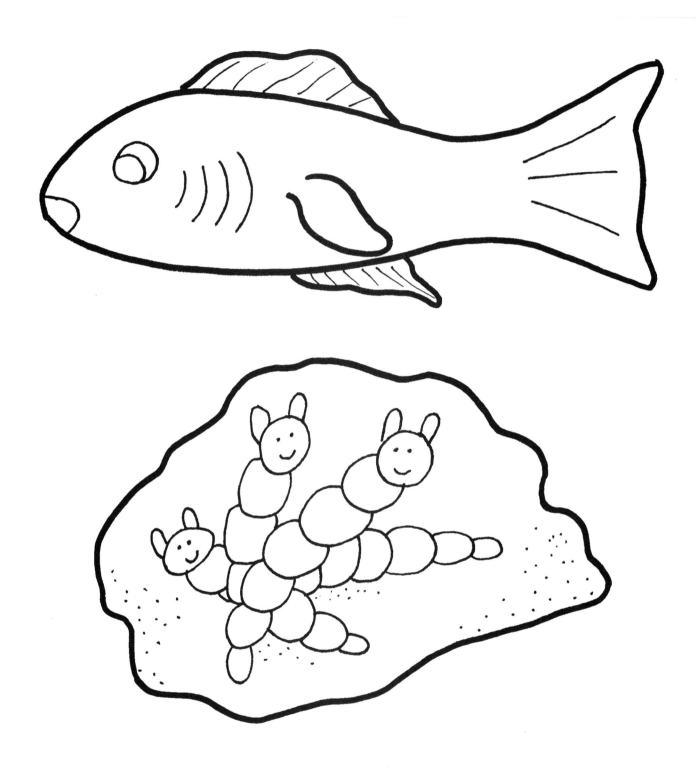

Figure 2.22 Patterns for Trout and Bugs in "Five Bear Cubs"

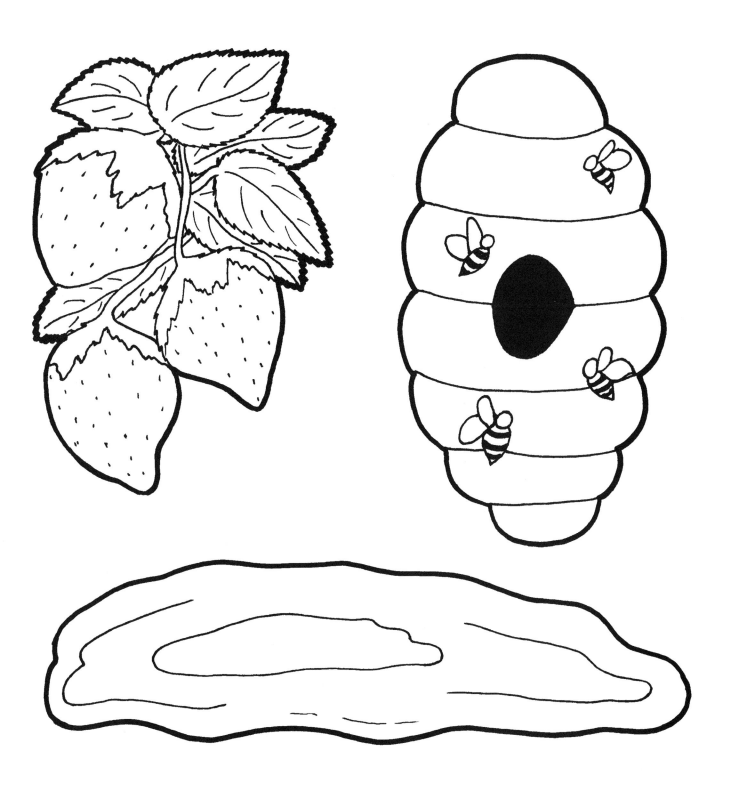

Figure 2.23 Pattern for Beehive, Strawberries, Water in "Five Bear Cubs"

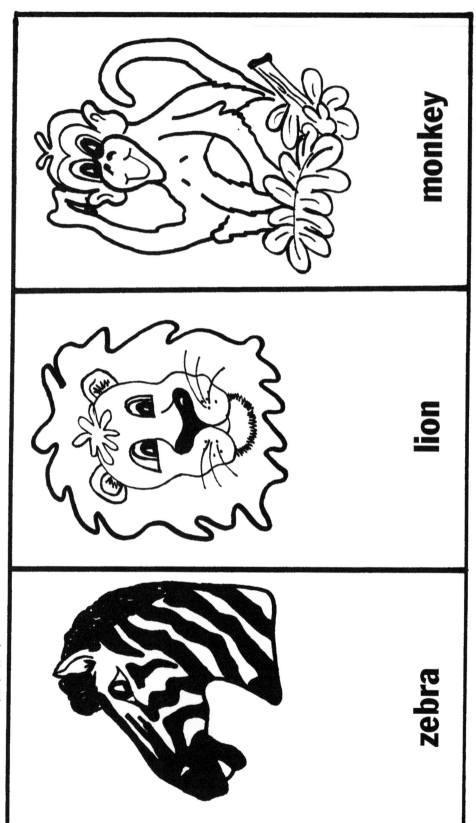

To Make Picture Cards:

Reproduce, color, and laminate the following pictures: alligator, fish, otter, lion, zebra, monkey, bat, bird, and bee.

Figure 2.24 Matching Activity Picture Cards

Figure 2.25 Matching Activity Picture Cards

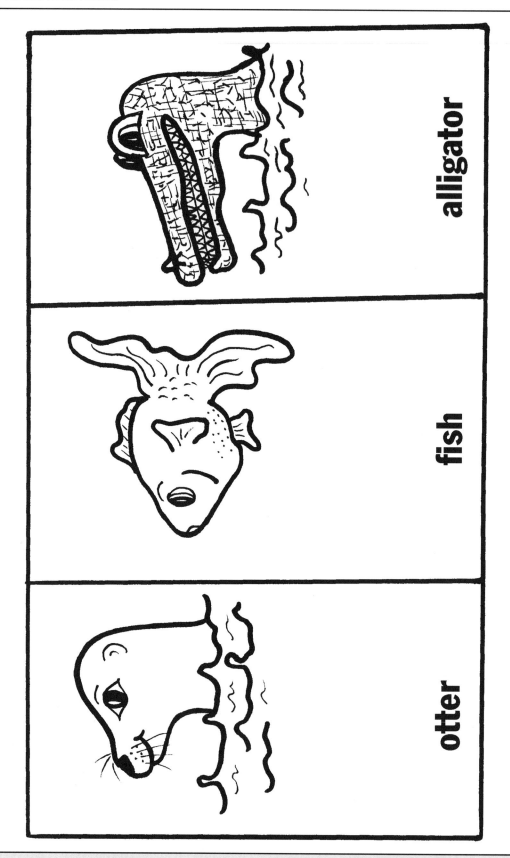

Figure 2.26 Matching Activity Picture Cards

1.

To Make a Three-Section Pocket:

1. Reproduce and color (don't laminate) the following pictures: land, sky, and water.
2. Laminate an 8½" × 11" piece of paper or card stock.
3. Fold in half lengthwise, leaving a one-inch difference in edges.
4. Staple vertically 3⅝" in from each side, creating three equal sections.
5. Glue the land picture, centered in the first section, the sky centered in the second section, and the water picture centered in the third section.
6. Cut a 15-inch strip of clear three-inch-wide book tape.
7. Center the tape over pictures before securing. Tape should overlap each side by two inches, then press tape into place, covering pictures and wrapping the two-inch excess around each end.

Figure 2.27 Instructions and Patterns for Matching Activity Pocket

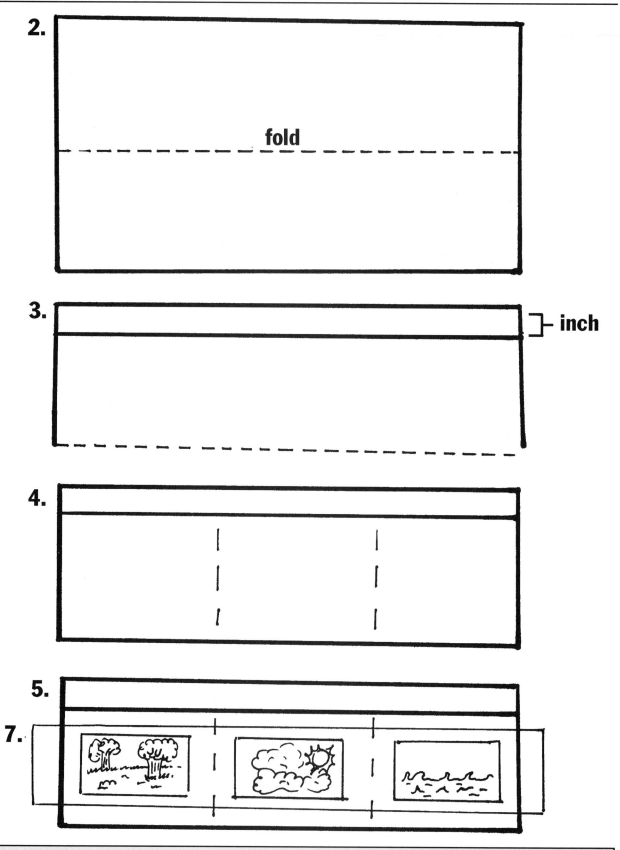

Figure 2.28 Instructions and Patterns for Matching Activity Pocket

five

To Prepare Pictures:

1. Purchase or bring from home a stuffed bear.
2. Color all patterns in colors of your choice.
3. Laminate.

5

Figure 2.29 Picture for "Berry Pickin' "

four

4

Figure 2.30 Picture for "Berry Pickin' "

three

3

Figure 2.31 Picture for "Berry Pickin' "

two

2

Figure 2.32 Picture for "Berry Pickin' "

one

1

Figure 2.33 Picture for "Berry Pickin' "

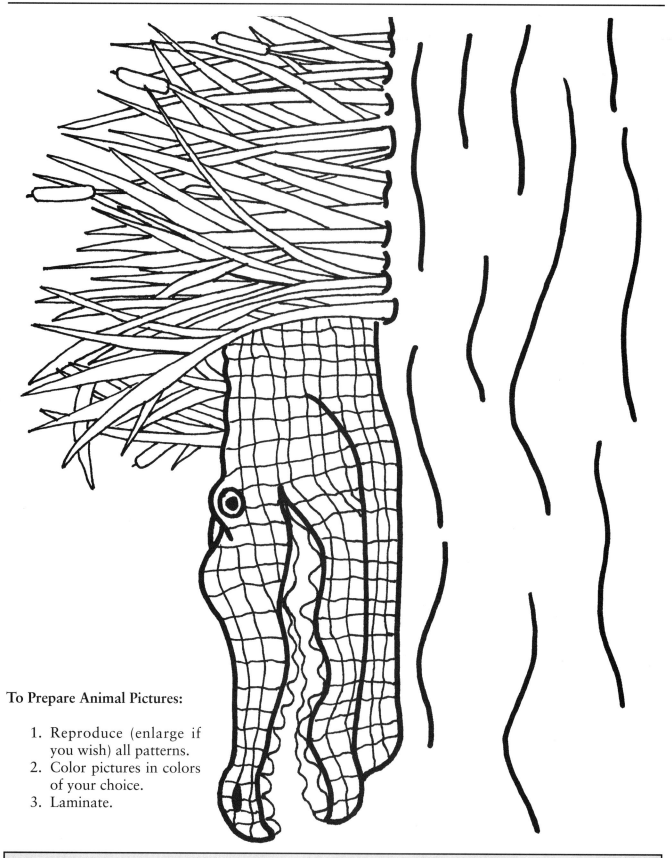

To Prepare Animal Pictures:

1. Reproduce (enlarge if you wish) all patterns.
2. Color pictures in colors of your choice.
3. Laminate.

Figure 2.34 Picture for "Let's Go for a Jungle Walk"

Figure 2.35 Picture for "Let's Go for a Jungle Walk"

Figure 2.36 Picture for "Let's Go for a Jungle Walk"

Figure 2.37 Picture for "Let's Go for a Jungle Walk"

Figure 2.38 Picture for "Let's Go for a Jungle Walk"

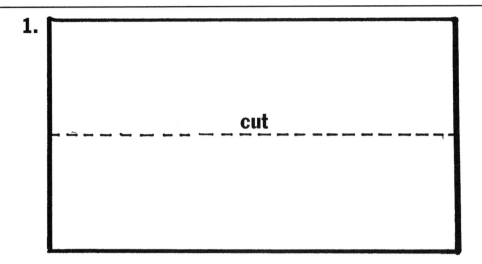

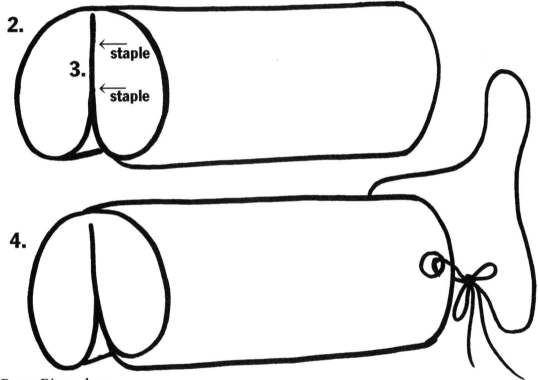

To Make Paper Binoculars:

Gather the following items: One piece of card stock (color of your choice) for every two pair of binoculars, hole punch, stapler, staples, and a piece of yarn 18 inches in length (color of your choice).

1. Cut card stock in half lengthwise.
2. Roll paper from each end to form two tubes.
3. Staple tubes in place.
4. Punch a hole at the top, outside edge of each tube to tie yarn (binoculars will hang around the neck).

Figure 2.39 Binoculars for "Let's Go for a Jungle Walk"

Figure 2.40 "We're Gonna Visit the Zoo" Coloring Sheet

bat

monkey

alligator

Wild Animal Concentration

To make a concentration game:
1. color pictures and cut apart
2. each child will need two sets of animal pictures

To play:
1. spread all cards face down on a flat surface
2. on each turn flip two cards over, revealing both animals
3. if they match, keep them, if they don't, flip them back over and wait for next turn
4. continue until all animals are matched

Figure 2.41 "Wild Animal Concentration" Activity Sheet

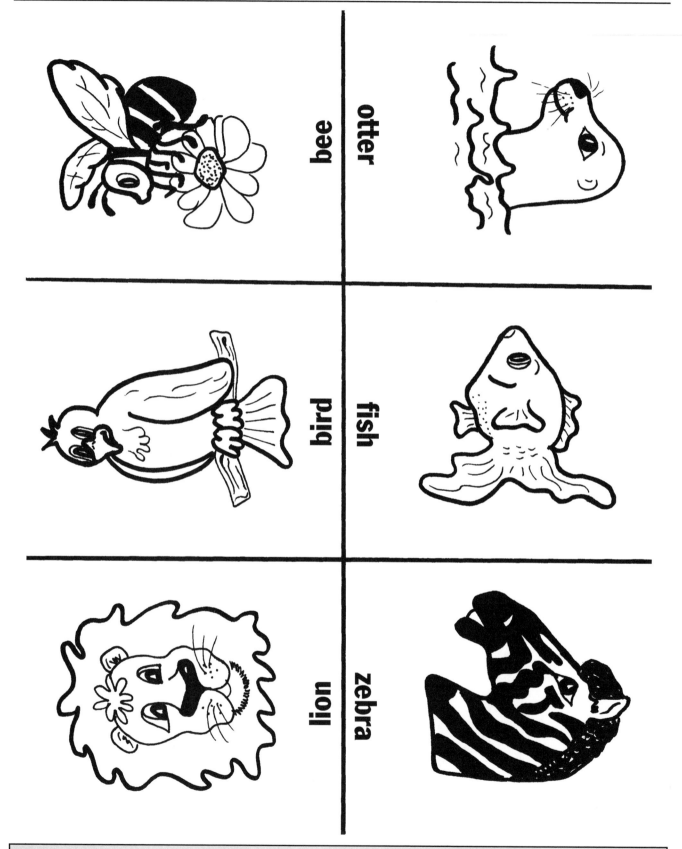

otter

bee

fish

bird

zebra

lion

Figure 2.42 "Wild Animal Concentration" Activity Sheet

CHAPTER THREE

Desert Dash

Desert Dash outline
Share sunny desert stories kids will bask in.

The Welcome Song page 107 (*song #1 from CD*)
Read-A-Loud page 108 (*book*)
One Tarantula page 108 (*fingerplay*)
Shady Hat pages 108 to 110 (*flannel or magnetic story*)
Five Little Coyotes pages 110 to 111 (*flannel or magnetic story, song #7 from CD*)
Toad's Trip pages 111 to 112 (*puppet story*)
This Little Bird pages 112 to 113 (*action song #8 from CD*)
Matching page 113 (*parent and child activity*)
The Stretch and Sit Song page 114 (*song #2 from CD*)
Five Black and Shiny Crows pages 114 to 115 (*flannel or magnetic story*)
Come Hike in the Desert pages 115 to 116 (*action song #9 from CD*)
Shady Hat Coloring Sheet page 116 (*handout*)
Five Little Coyote Finger Puppets Activity Sheet page 116 (*handout*)

THE WELCOME SONG

(*play song #1 from CD to let children know you are ready to begin*)
Let's begin our storytime, see a play, and hear a rhyme. Welcome mom and daddy too, they can sit right next to you. Songs to sing and books to see, you'll have fun each week with me.

READ-A-LOUD BOOK

Choose a book related to deserts; we recommend reading Dig, Wait, Listen: A Desert Toad's Tale *by April Pulley Sayre, illustrated by Barbara Bash (New York: Greenwillow Books, 2001).*

ONE TARANTULA

Here comes one tarantula.
> *(hold right hand with palm down, wiggle fingers, "walking" on opposite hand's fingertips)*

Here come two owls,
> *(make circles with hands and place around eyes every time you say the word owls)*

and one tarantula.
> *(hold right hand with palm down, wiggle fingers, "walking" on opposite hand from fingertips to wrist)*

Here come three coyotes,
> *(tip head back and howl every time you say the word coyotes)*

two owls, and one tarantula.
> *(hold right hand with palm down, wiggle fingers, "walking" on opposite arm from wrist to elbow)*

Here come four snakes,
> *(wiggle index finger and hiss every time you say the word snakes)*

three coyotes, two owls, and one tarantula.
> *(hold right hand with palm down, wiggle fingers, "walking" on opposite arm from elbow to shoulder)*

Here come five crows,
> *(flap arms to resemble a bird's wings and say, "caw, caw")*

four snakes, three coyotes, two owls, and one tarantula.
> *(hold right hand with palm down, wiggle fingers, "walking" on opposite arm from shoulder to neck, look at pretend tarantula and scream)*

SHADY HAT

> *(encourage children to join you when saying, "Imagine that! He grabbed the hat!" children also enjoy adding the following actions: "Imagine that!"— shrug shoulders; "He grabbed the hat!"—hug self)*

Bobcat sat in the sun wearing his brand new shade hat.
> *(place bobcat, wearing hat, on far left side of board)*

He smiled because it was a special hat with a secret inside. "Shhhhhh."
Along came coyote.

(place coyote to right of bobcat)
Coyote took one look at the hat and howled, "Ahwoooo."
"I want a hat just like that!" and he grabbed the hat and plopped it on his head.
(remove hat from bobcat and place on coyote)
Bobcat said, "WAIT!," but it was just too late. Coyote howled again, "Ahwooo."
Imagine that! He grabbed the hat!
Along came snake.
(place snake to right of coyote)
Snake took one look at the hat and hissed, "Sssss."
"I want a hat just like that!" and he grabbed the hat and plopped it on his head.
(remove hat from coyote and place on snake)
Bobcat said, "WAIT!" but it was just too late. Snake hissed again, "Sssssss."
Imagine that! He grabbed the hat!
Along came toad.
(place toad to right of snake)
Toad took one look at the hat and croaked, "Ribbit, ribbit."
"I want a hat just like that!" and he grabbed the hat and plopped it on his head.
(remove hat from snake and place on toad)
Bobcat said, "WAIT!" but it was just too late. Toad croaked again, "Ribbit, ribbit."
Imagine that! He grabbed the hat!
Along came owl.
(place owl to right of toad)
Owl took one look at the hat and hooted, "Whooo, whooo."
"I want a hat just like that!" and he grabbed the hat and plopped it on his head.
(remove hat from toad and place on owl)
Bobcat said, "WAIT!" but it was just too late. Owl hooted again, "Whooo, whooo."
Imagine that! He grabbed the hat!
BUZZZZZZZ
(make loud buzzing sound)
Owl said, "Whooo, whooo! Imagine that! A buzzing hat! I don't want that!"
Owl gave the hat back to toad.
(remove hat from owl and place on toad)
Toad said, "Ribbit, ribbit! Imagine that! A buzzing hat! I don't want that!"
Toad gave the hat back to snake.
(remove hat from toad and place on snake)

Snake said, "Sssssss! Imagine that! A buzzing hat! I don't want that!"
Snake gave the hat back to coyote.

(*remove hat from snake and place on coyote*)

Coyote said, "Ahwooo! Imagine that! A buzzing hat! I don't want that!"
Coyote gave the hat back to bobcat.

(*remove hat from coyote and place on bobcat*)

Bobcat just smiled as he listened to his buzzing hat. Then he said, "Yes, my hat is quite special. Imagine if you can, how a bee's buzzing wings make a very cool fan!"

(*place bee on bobcat's hat*)

To make as a flannel story: (see figures 3.1, 3.2, 3.3, 3.4, 3.5, and 3.6, pages 118 to 123)

To make as a magnetic story: (see figures 3.1, 3.2, 3.3, 3.4, 3.5, and 3.6, pages 118 to 123)

FIVE LITTLE COYOTES

(*before you begin, place the moon and one coyote on the board, then play song #7 from CD*)

One little coyote howling at the moon, along came a friend and joined in his tune.

(*place second coyote on board*)

Two little coyotes howling at the moon, along came a friend and joined in his tune.

(*place third coyote on board*)

Three little coyotes howling at the moon, along came a friend and joined in his tune.

(*place fourth coyote on board*)

Four little coyotes howling at the moon, along came a friend and joined in his tune.

(*place fifth coyote on board*)

Five little coyotes howling at the moon, along came a friend and joined in his tune.

(*walk in place swinging arms*)

Five wild coyotes watch an owl soar, one ran after it and then there were four.

(*remove one coyote from board*)

Four wild coyotes sniffing at a tree, one chased a mouse and then there were three.

(*remove second coyote from board*)

Three wild coyotes where the clover grew, one saw a butterfly and then there were two.

(*remove third coyote from board*)

Two wild coyotes sitting in the sun, one went for a drink and then there was one.
(remove fourth coyote from board)
One wild coyote howling at the moon, he went to sleep 'cause the sun would be up soon.
(remove fifth coyote from board)

To make as a flannel story: (see figures 3.7 and 3.8, pages 124 and 125)

To make as a magnetic story: (see figures 3.7 and 3.8, pages 124 and 125)

TOAD'S TRIP

(toad puppet on stage)
Toad woke up one morning and said, "Enough of this heat, I'm going to the beach!"
He grabbed his beach towel and set off.
(place beach towel on toad)
Along the way, he met his friend Javelina.
(javelina puppet enters and says)
"Hey Toad where are you going?"
(Toad)
"I've had enough of this heat, I'm going to the beach!"
(Javelina)
"The beach, it's a long way away, Toad. If you're going to go that far, you better take a cup of water. Here you can have mine."
(place glass next to toad)
(Toad hopping)
"Thanks Javelina! See ya."
(javelina puppet exits)
A little further down the road, Toad met his friend Jackrabbit.
(jackrabbit puppet enters and says)
"Hi Toad, where are you going?"
(Toad)
"I've had enough of this heat, I'm going to the beach!"
(Jackrabbit)
"The beach, it's a long way away, Toad. If you're going to go that far, you better take an umbrella. Here you can have mine."
(place umbrella next to Toad)
(Toad hopping)
"Thanks Jackrabbit! See ya."
(jackrabbit puppet exits)
Still further down the road, Toad met his friend Snake.
(snake puppet enters and says)

"Hey Toad where are you going?"
　　(Toad)
"I've had enough of this heat, I'm going to the beach!"
　　(Snake)
"The beach, it's a long way away, Toad. If you're going to go that far, you better take some lunch. Here you can have mine."
　　(Toad hopping)
"Thanks Snake! See ya."
　　(snake puppet exits)
Way down the road, Toad didn't see anyone.
　　(Toad looks around and says)
"Wow, I'm really getting hot, I think I need to rest awhile."
　　(Toad hops a little more then says)
"Here's a nice spot, I think I'll put up my umbrella."
　　(open umbrella)
　　(Toad)
"The sand sure is hot, I think I'll sit on my beach towel."
　　(spread beach towel under umbrella and place toad puppet on beach towel)
　　(Toad)
"A little food,
　　(make munching sound)
a sip of water."
　　(make slurping sound)
"Ahhhhhh, life doesn't get any better than this! Who needs the beach?"
　　(Toad pauses, then slowly says with emphasis)
"The beach, it's a lo-ng way away!"

To use as a puppet story you will need to gather the following items: a small umbrella, washcloth (for beach towel), small plastic glass, brown paper bag with the edge folded over. The following puppets are needed: toad, snake, javelina, and jackrabbit. If you don't own these puppets, follow the instructions (see pages 126, 131, 135, and 139), using the patterns provided to create your own.

THIS LITTLE BIRD

(play song #8 from CD)
(before you begin show children how to use their hands to resemble a bird flying; make "bird hands" by crossing thumbs connecting them, then wave hands; make this motion very time you sing the words, "This little bird")
This little bird, began to roam, looking for a place to call his home.
　　(shade eyes with hand and look around)

with a hip-hop, flippity-flop, now he's on his way,
>	(*hop on right foot; then hop on left; jump forward twice, then wave good-bye; repeat this action every time you sing the phrase, "with a hip-hop, flippity-flop, now he's on his way*)
this little bird set off today.
This little bird, he flew north,
>	(*move "bird hands" upward*)
rained so hard he zipped back and forth,
>	(*with thumbs still connected, wiggle fingers to resemble rain, then make the letter Z in the air*)
with a hip-hop, flippity-flop, now he's on his way, this little bird flew north today.
This little bird, he flew east
>	(*move "bird hands" left*)
carrying a knapsack with a feast,
>	(*pretend to throw knapsack over shoulder*)
with a hip-hop, flippity-flop, now he's on his way, this little bird flew east today.
This little bird, he flew south
>	(*move "bird hands" downward*)
holding a suitcase in his mouth,
>	(*using both hands, pretend to hold a suitcase handle up to mouth*)
with a hip-hop, flippity-flop, now he's on his way, this little bird flew south today.
This little bird, he flew west,
>	(*move "bird hands" right*)
found a sunny Arizona nest,
>	(*cup hands to make a nest*)
with a hip-hop, flippity-flop, he's not goin' away,
>	(*shake head no*)
this little bird is here to stay.
>	(*cup left hand, then point with right index finger into left palm*)

MATCHING

A packet, with four picture cards, cut in half, is given to each child. The child and parent work together matching the two halves to complete each picture. Make one packet for every child. Each packet will consist of four pictures and a pocket to put them in.

To make picture cards: (see figure 3.23, page 144)

To make a pocket: (see figure 3.24, page 145)

THE STRETCH AND SIT SONG

(play song #2 from CD)
Let's stand up together. Now let's all touch our nose. Put our hands in the air high, bend down, and touch our toes. Let's stand up together. Now let's all touch our nose. Put our hands in the air high, bend down, and touch our toes. Now it's time to listen so sit right on the floor. Hands are in our laps now and we are ready for more.

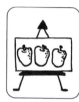

FIVE BLACK AND SHINY CROWS

(can be sung to the tune of "Five Freckled Frogs")
(before you begin, place hose on board with all five crows sitting on it)
Five black and shiny crows sat on a garden hose, watching the water sprinkle down. Caw! Caw! One jumped into the spray where he could play all day.
(remove one crow from board)
Now there are four black shiny crows. Caw! Caw!
Four black and shiny crows sat on a garden hose, watching the water sprinkle down. Caw! Caw! One jumped into the spray where he could play all day.
Now there are three black shiny crows. Caw! Caw!
(remove another crow)
Three black and shiny crows sat on a garden hose, watching the water sprinkle down. Caw! Caw! One jumped into the spray where he could play all day.
Now there are two black shiny crows. Caw! Caw!
(remove another crow)
Two black and shiny crows sat on a garden hose, watching the water sprinkle down. Caw! Caw! One jumped into the spray where he could play all day.
Now there is one black shiny crow. Caw! Caw!
(remove another crow)
One black and shiny crow sat on a garden hose, watching the water sprinkle down. Caw! Caw! He jumped into the spray where he could play all day.
Now there are no black shiny crows. Caw! Caw!
(remove last crow)

To make as a flannel story: (see figure 3.25, page 146)

To make a garden hose:
  1. Cut one green felt square into one-inch strips.

2. *Glue strips end-to-end to span flannel board.*
3. *Enhance with felt markers.*

To make as a magnetic story: (see figure 3.25, page 146)

To make a garden hose:
1. *Paint a yardstick green and let dry.*
2. *Enhance with markers.*
3. *Attach magnets to back.*

COME HIKE IN THE DESERT

(*have children stand up, give each child an aluminum pie plate, then play song #9 from CD*)
Come hike in the desert,
(*beckon with hand every time you sing the phrase, "Come hike in the desert"*)
and have some fun with me.
(*point to self every time you sing the phrase, "and have some fun with me*)
Place a hat upon your head to shade it from the sun.
(*hold pie plate on head every time you sing the phrase, "shade it from the sun"*)
Come hike in the desert, and have some fun with me.
In rocks and water search for gold, panning is such fun,
(*hold pie plate in front of you, move hands in circular motion pretending to swish water every time you sing the phrase, "panning is such fun"*)
shade it from the sun.
Come hike in the desert and have some fun with me.
The tortoise moves so slowly, when he tries to run,
(*invert pie plate and rock it side to side every time you sing the phrase, "when he tries to run"*)
panning is such fun, shade it from the sun.
Come hike in the desert and have some fun with me.
I really wish the wind would blow when it's 1–0–1,
(*fan self with pie plate every time you sing the phrase, "when it's 1–0–1"*)
when he tries to run, panning is such fun, shade it from the sun.
Come hike in the desert and have some fun with me.
Roasting hot dogs on a fire, I like mine well done,
(*hold plate with arms outstretched, then pull plate toward you*)
when it's 1–0–1, when he tries to run, panning is such fun, shade it from the sun.

Come hike in the desert and have some fun with me.
I think I hear a rattlesnake, rattling in the sun!
 (*tap fingernails on pie plate*)
YES! I hear a rattlesnake, now it's time to run!

SHADY HAT COLORING SHEET

(*see figure 3.26, page 147*)

FIVE LITTLE COYOTE FINGER PUPPETS ACTIVITY SHEET

(*see figure 3.27, page 148*)

"Desert Dash" Support Materials

To Make as a Flannel Story:

1. Cut all patterns from felt colors of your choice.
2. Enhance with felt markers.

To Make as a Magnetic Story

1. Reproduce patterns.
2. Color all patterns in colors of your choice.
3. Laminate.
4. Cut out.
5. Attach a magnetic strip to the back of each piece.

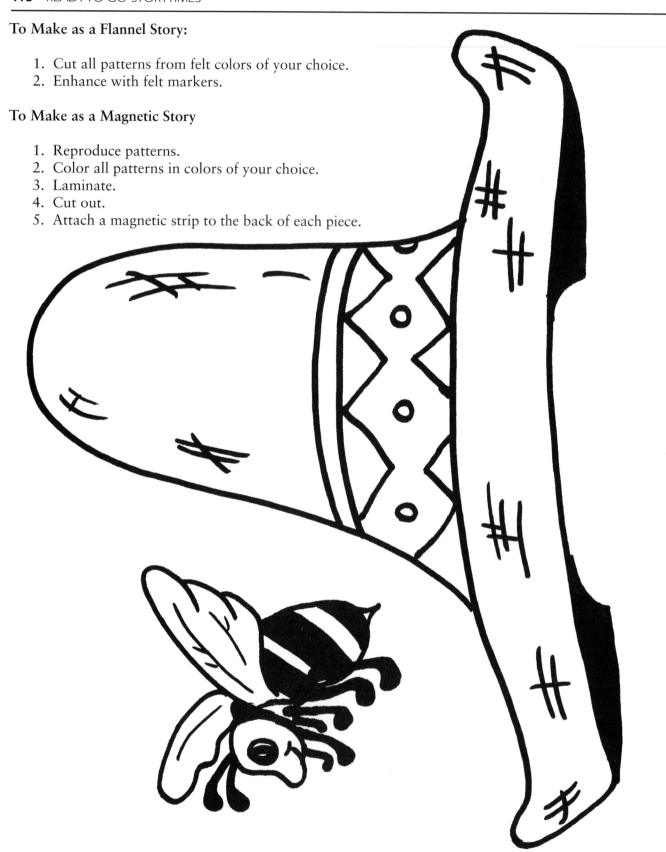

Figure 3.1 Hat and Bee Patterns for "Shady Hat"

Figure 3.2 Bobcat Pattern for "Shady Hat"

Figure 3.3 Coyote Pattern for "Shady Hat"

Figure 3.4 Toad Pattern for "Shady Hat"

Figure 3.5 Owl Pattern for "Shady Hat"

Figure 3.6 Snake Pattern for "Shady Hat"

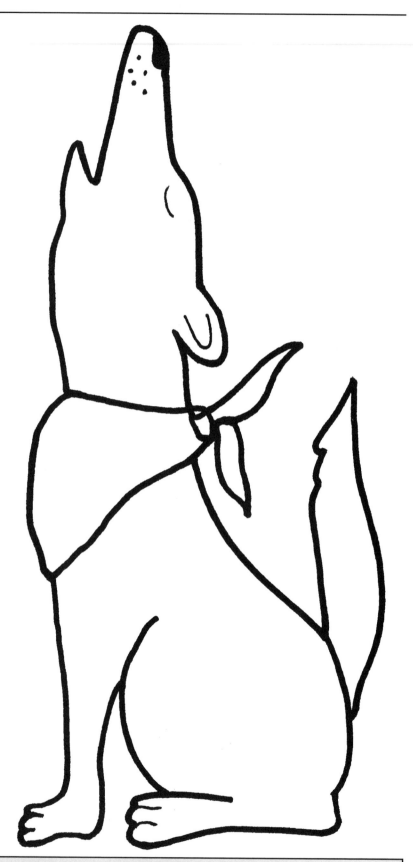

To Make as a Flannel Story:

1. Cut moon pattern from yellow felt.
2. Reproduce coyote pattern five times and cut from felt colors of your choice.
3. Enhance with felt markers.

To Make as a Magnetic Story:

1. Reproduce moon pattern once and coyote pattern five times.
2. Color all pictures in colors of your choice.
3. Laminate.
4. Cut out.
5. Attach a magnetic strip to the back of each piece.

Figure 3.7 Coyote Pattern for "Five Little Coyotes"

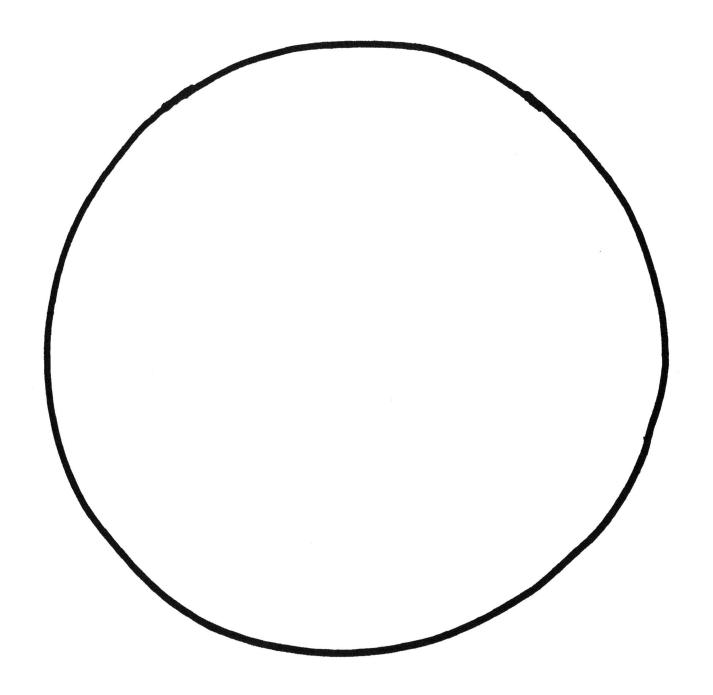

Figure 3.8 Moon Pattern for "Five Little Coyotes"

Toad Puppet for "Toad's Trip"

Materials needed:

- three pieces of olive felt
- one-half piece of brown felt
- one-fourth piece of pink felt
- two, two-inch light brown pompoms
- two, one-inch "googly" eyes
- one 5" × 7" piece of card stock (any color)
- needle and olive thread
- one toilet paper roll
- white glue
- scissors

To assemble: (*see figures 3.9, 3.10, 3.11, and 3.12, pages 127 to 130*)

Enlarge all patterns on photocopier by 115% or more to best suit your hand-size.

1. Cut out mouth insert, from card stock, and set aside.
2. Cut out all pattern pieces, in felt colors as marked, and set aside.
3. Fold mouth piece in half and place on top of large body piece marked "A" (matching A ends).
4. Sew the mouth to the body, stopping at the fold.
5. Place the other body piece, marked "B," on top of the other side of the mouth piece (matching B ends)
6. Sew the mouth to the body, stopping at the fold.
7. Sew short legs one-half inch from the front of the puppet, marked "X."
8. Sew long legs one inch from back of the puppet, marked "XXX" and finish side seams.
9. Glue brown spots randomly to legs and back.
10. Place glue inside each end of toilet paper roll and on half (lengthwise) of the outside of the roll.
11. Insert into mouth area "A," glue side down, and tuck felt (toad's "cheeks") into each end of the toilet paper roll forming a dimpled look.
12. Place glue on the top side of the card stock and insert into the mouth section "B," glue side up.
13. Glue tongue into mouth at "C."
14. Sew light brown pompoms to the top of head, marked "xx."
15. Glue "googly" eyes to the front of each pompom.
16. Glue nose holes into place.
17. When inserting your hand into the toad puppet, your fingers will be on the top side of the toilet paper roll and your thumb under the card stock insert.

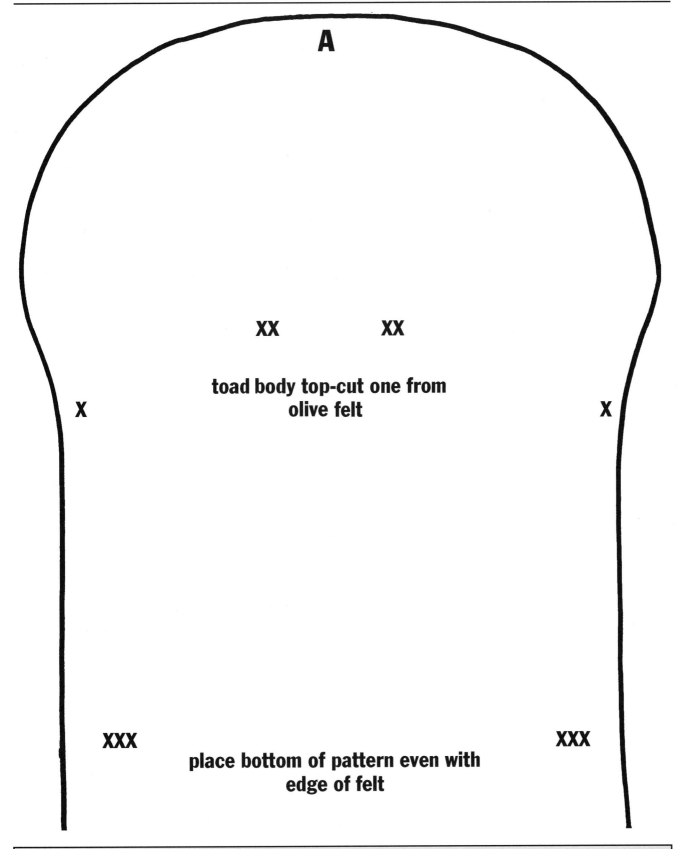

A

XX   XX

**toad body top-cut one from
olive felt**

X   X

XXX   XXX

**place bottom of pattern even with
edge of felt**

Figure 3.9 Pattern for Toad Puppet

B

**toad body bottom-cut one
from olive felt**

**place bottom of pattern even with
edge of felt**

Figure 3.10 Pattern for Toad Puppet

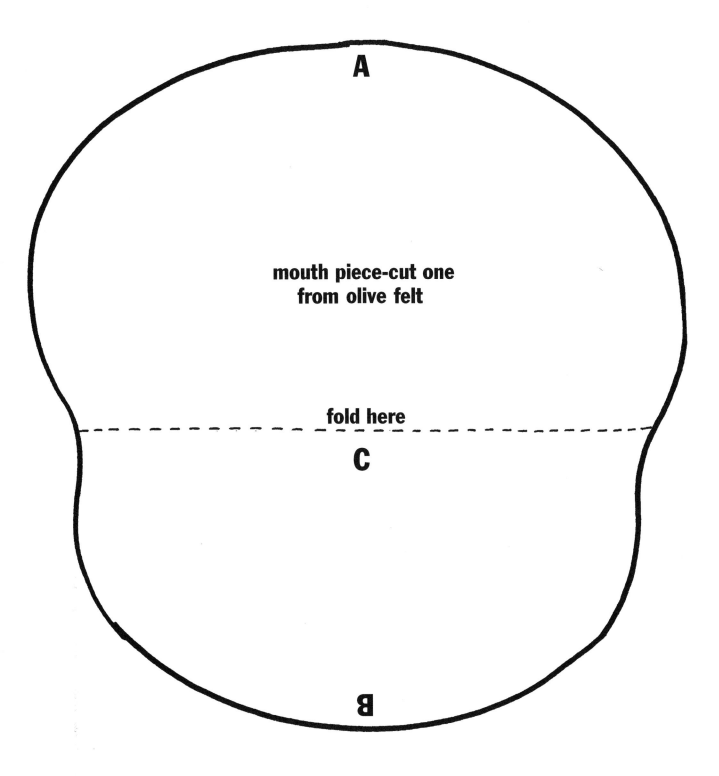

A

**mouth piece-cut one
from olive felt**

fold here

C

B

Figure 3.11 Pattern for Toad Puppet

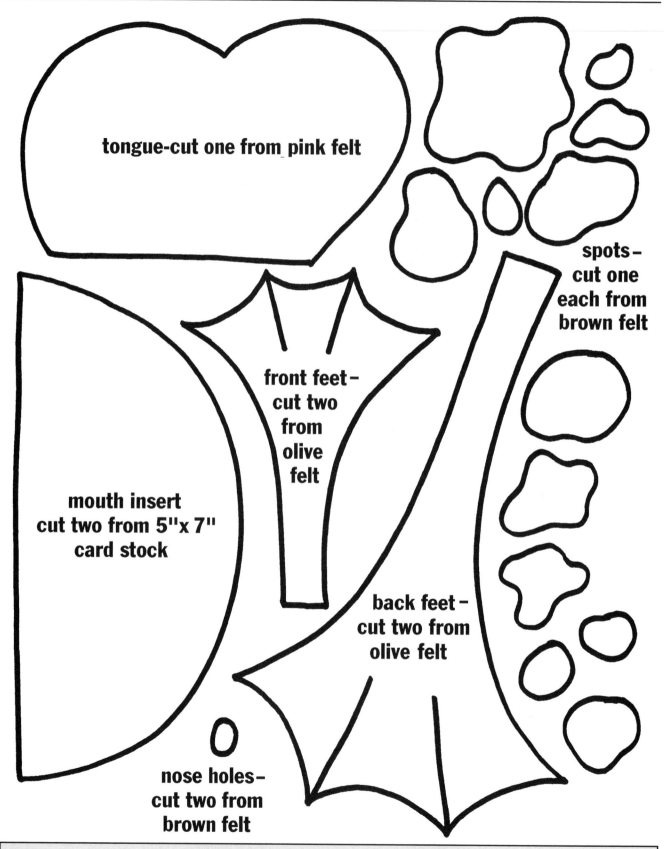

tongue-cut one from pink felt

spots–
cut one
each from
brown felt

front feet–
cut two
from
olive
felt

mouth insert
cut two from 5"x 7"
card stock

back feet–
cut two from
olive felt

nose holes–
cut two from
brown felt

Figure 3.12 Patterns for Toad Puppet

Snake Puppet for "Toad's Trip"

Materials needed:

- three pieces of black felt
- one piece of red felt
- one piece of yellow felt
- one toilet paper roll
- one 5" × 7" piece of card stock (any color)
- six, one-half inch black pompoms
- white glue
- needle and black thread
- stapler
- scissors

To assemble: (*see drawings 3.13, 3.14, and 3.15, pages 132 to 134***)**

Enlarge all patterns on photocopier by 115% or more to best suit your hand-size.

1. Cut out mouth insert, from card stock, and set aside.
2. Cut out all pattern pieces, in colors as marked, and set aside.
3. Fold mouth piece in half and place on top of body piece marked "A" (matching A ends).
4. Sew the mouth to the body, stopping at the fold.
5. Place the other body piece on top of mouth piece, marked "B" (matching B ends).
6. Sew the mouth to the body, stopping at the fold.
7. Sew stripes to main body (top and bottom) marked "Y" for yellow, "R" for red and "BB" for black (color order—yellow, red, yellow, black) and finish side seams.
8. Glue three pompoms together forming a pyramid.
9. Glue felt eyes to front of pompom pyramid.
10. Glue completed eyes in place, marked "xx."
11. Cut two inches off end of toilet paper roll and discard; staple closed one end of remaining half.
12. Place glue over entire roll and insert into mouth section "A," with stapled end first.
13. Place glue on the top side of the card stock and insert into mouth section "B," glue side up.
14. Glue tongue into mouth.
15. When inserting your hand into the snake puppet, three of your fingers will be in the toilet paper roll; your thumb will be under the card stock insert, in the bottom portion of the snake's mouth.

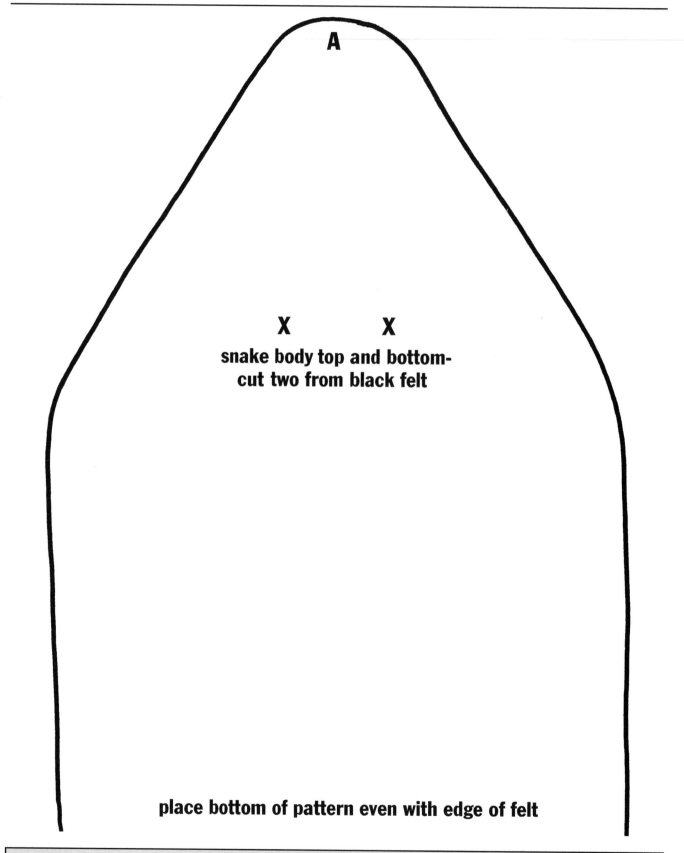

A

X   **X**

**snake body top and bottom–
cut two from black felt**

place bottom of pattern even with edge of felt

Figure 3.13 Pattern for Snake Puppet

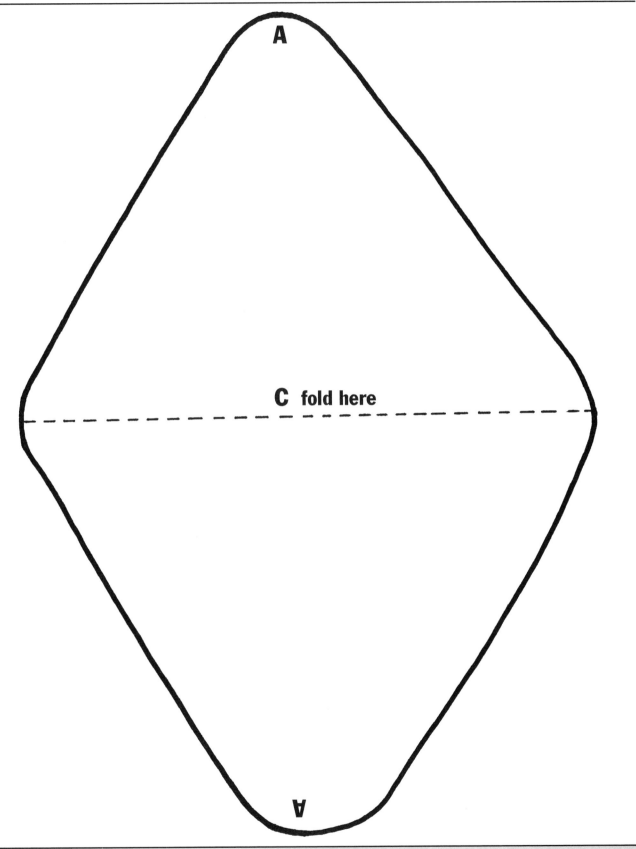

A

C fold here

ᐯ

Figure 3.14 Pattern for Snake Puppet

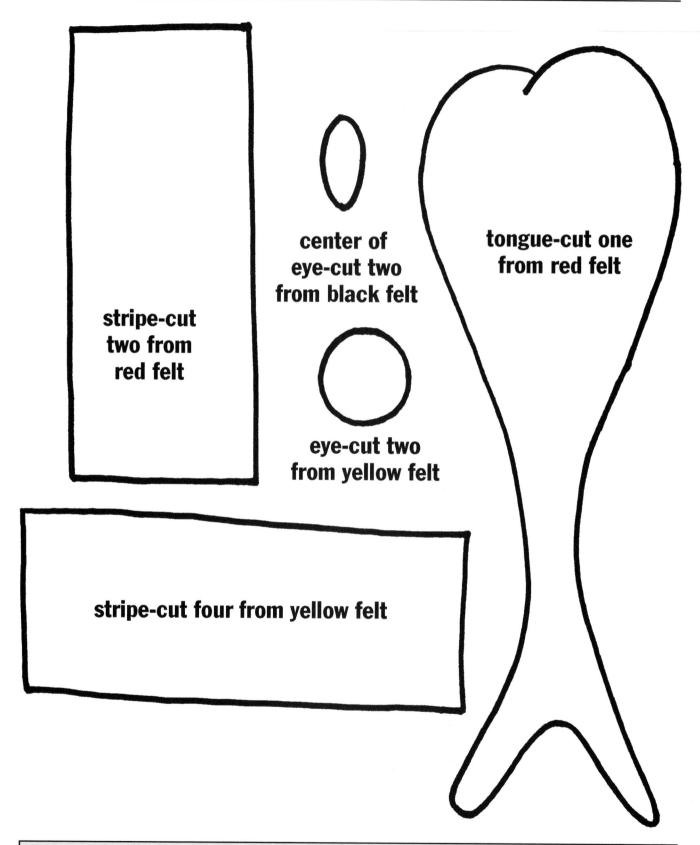

stripe-cut
two from
red felt

center of
eye-cut two
from black felt

eye-cut two
from yellow felt

tongue-cut one
from red felt

stripe-cut four from yellow felt

Figure 3.15 Pattern Pieces for Snake Puppet

Javelina Puppet for "Toad's Trip"

Materials needed:

- three pieces of gray or charcoal felt
- one-half piece of black felt
- one-fourth piece of white felt
- one 5" × 7" piece of card stock (any color)
- one ten-ounce Styrofoam cup
- white glue
- needle and gray or charcoal thread
- scissors

To assemble: (see *figures 3.16, 3.17, and 3.18, pages 136 to 138*)

Enlarge all patterns on photocopier by 115% or more to best suit your hand-size.

1. Cut Styrofoam cup in half lengthwise and set aside.
2. Cut out mouth insert, from card stock, and set aside.
3. Cut out all pattern pieces, in colors as marked, and set aside.
4. Sew the round end of the javelina snout, marked "a," to the small slightly curved end, marked "a" on the body pattern (matching a ends).
5. Repeat above step for the other body half and snout pieces.
6. Fold mouth piece in half and place on top of body piece marked "A" (matching A ends).
7. Sew the mouth to the body, stopping at the fold.
8. Place the other body piece, marked "B," on top of the other side of the mouth piece (matching B ends)
9. Sew the mouth to the body, stopping at the fold.
10. Sew two legs one inch from the front of the puppet and two legs one inch from the back of the puppet, marked "X," and finish side seams.
11. Sew tusks one inch from the end of the bottom jaw, with tusk's point facing toward the eyes.
12. Glue hooves on feet.
13. Place glue on one side of the card stock and insert into the bottom of mouth section "A," glue side down.
14. Place glue on the outside of a Styrofoam cup half and glue into the top of mouth section "A," glue side up.
15. Place glue on one side of the other piece of card stock and insert into the top of mouth section "B," glue side up.
16. Place glue on the outside of remaining Styrofoam cup half and glue into the bottom of mouth section "B," glue side down.
17. Sew ears to the top of the puppet's head, marked "D."
18. Glue eyes in place, marked "xx."
19. Glue nose holes in place, marked by "t."

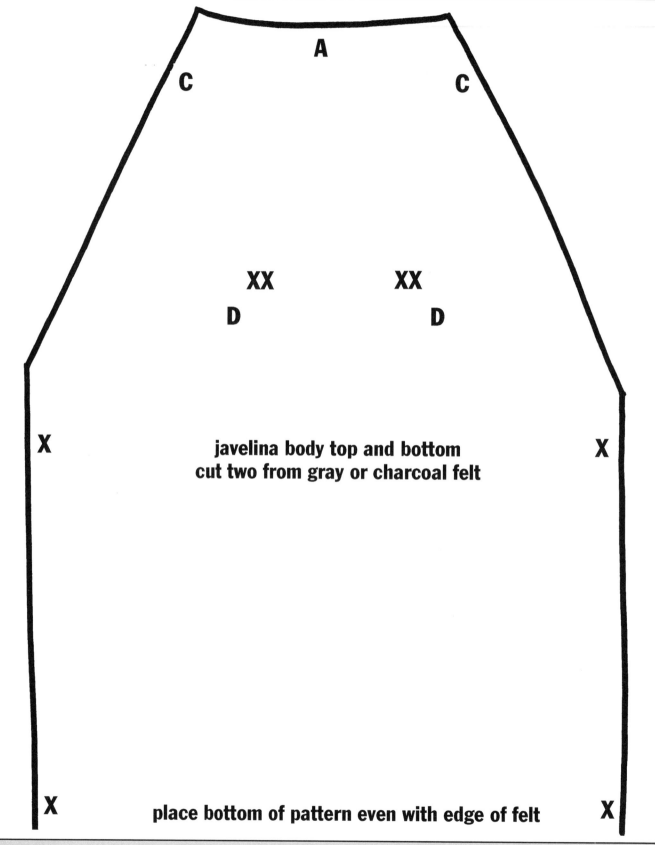

A

C   C

XX   XX

D   D

X   X

javelina body top and bottom
cut two from gray or charcoal felt

X   place bottom of pattern even with edge of felt   X

Figure 3.16 Pattern for Javelina Puppet

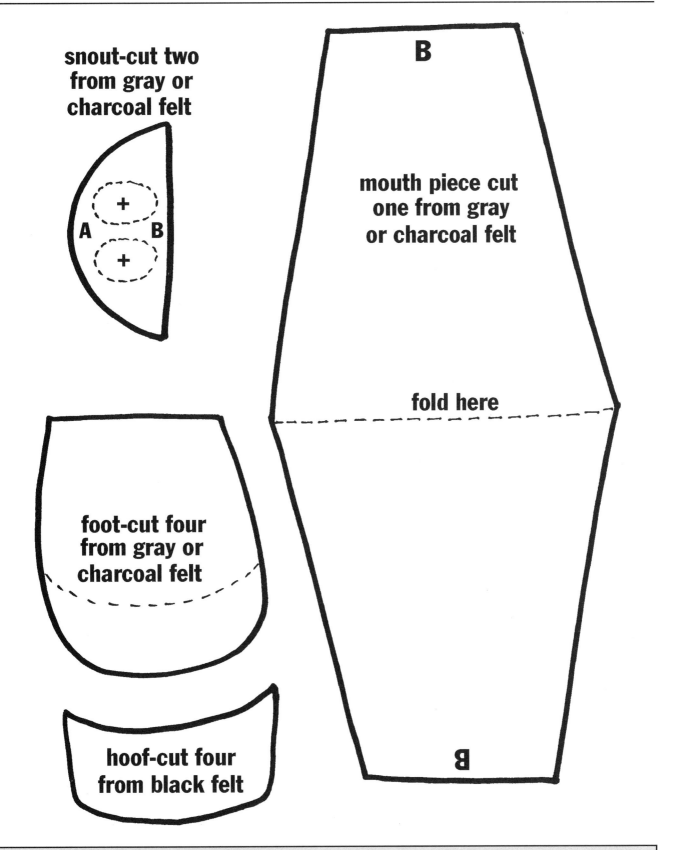

snout-cut two from gray or charcoal felt

A   B

mouth piece cut one from gray or charcoal felt

B

fold here

foot-cut four from gray or charcoal felt

hoof-cut four from black felt

B

Figure 3.17 Pattern Pieces for Javelina Puppet

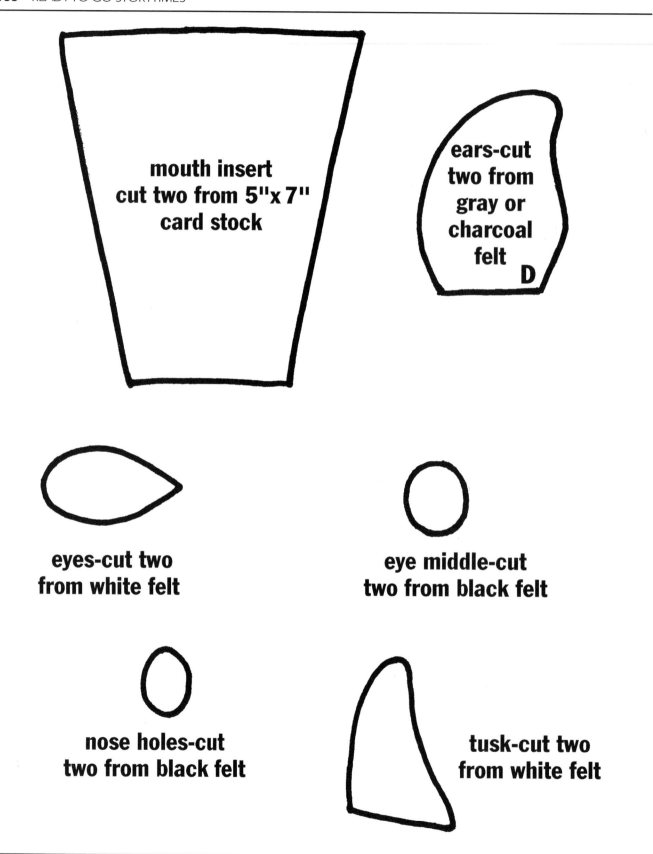

mouth insert
cut two from 5"x 7"
card stock

ears-cut
two from
gray or
charcoal
felt
D

eyes-cut two
from white felt

eye middle-cut
two from black felt

nose holes-cut
two from black felt

tusk-cut two
from white felt

Figure 3.18 Pattern Pieces for Javelina Puppet

Jackrabbit Puppet for "Toad's Trip"

Materials needed:

- two and one-half pieces of tan felt
- one-half piece of pink felt
- one-eighth piece of white felt
- one yard black embroidery floss
- two, one-half inch tan pompoms
- two, one-half inch "googly" eyes
- one 8½" × 11" piece of card stock (any color)
- needle and tan thread
- small amount of fiber fill or batting
- white glue
- toilet paper roll
- scissors

To assemble: (*see figures 3.19, 3.20, 3.21, and 3.22, pages 140 to 143*)

Enlarge all patterns on photocopier by 115% or more to best suit your hand-size.

1. Cut out mouth inserts, from card stock, and set aside.
2. Cut out all pattern pieces, in colors as marked, and set aside.
3. Fold mouth piece in half and place on top of body piece marked "A" (matching A ends)
4. Sew the mouth to the body, stopping at the fold.
5. Place the other body piece, marked "B," on top of the other side of the mouth piece (matching B ends)
6. Sew the mouth to the body, stopping at the fold.
7. Sew feet one inch from the front of puppet, marked "X," and finish side seams.
8. Place glue on one side of card stock and insert into mouth section "A," glue side down.
9. Place glue on one side of remaining card stock and insert into mouth section "B," glue side up.
10. Place a small amount (size of half dollar) of fiber fill into the end of the jackrabbit's nose, mouth piece "A."
11. Cut one third off end of toilet paper roll and discard remaining two-thirds roll.
12. Place glue over entire roll and insert firmly against fiber fill in the end of mouth section "A."
13. Place a small amount of fiber fill on either side of toilet paper roll.
14. When inserting your hand into the jackrabbit puppet, three of your fingers will be in the toilet paper roll; your thumb will be under the card stock insert, in the bottom portion of the jackrabbit's mouth.
15. Glue tongue into mouth at "C."
16. Glue pink ear pieces, centered on top of tan ear pieces, using plenty of glue, and let dry.
17. Sew ears to top of puppet's head, marked "D."
18. Press nose in slightly, creating a flat surface to attach nose and teeth.
19. Cut embroidery floss into six, six-inch pieces (whiskers will each be three inches long).
20. Sew in place on both sides of nose; pull ends of floss even; tie a knot to secure.
21. Glue on nose and teeth.
22. Glue pompoms in place, marked "xx."
23. Glue "googly" eyes to front of pompoms.

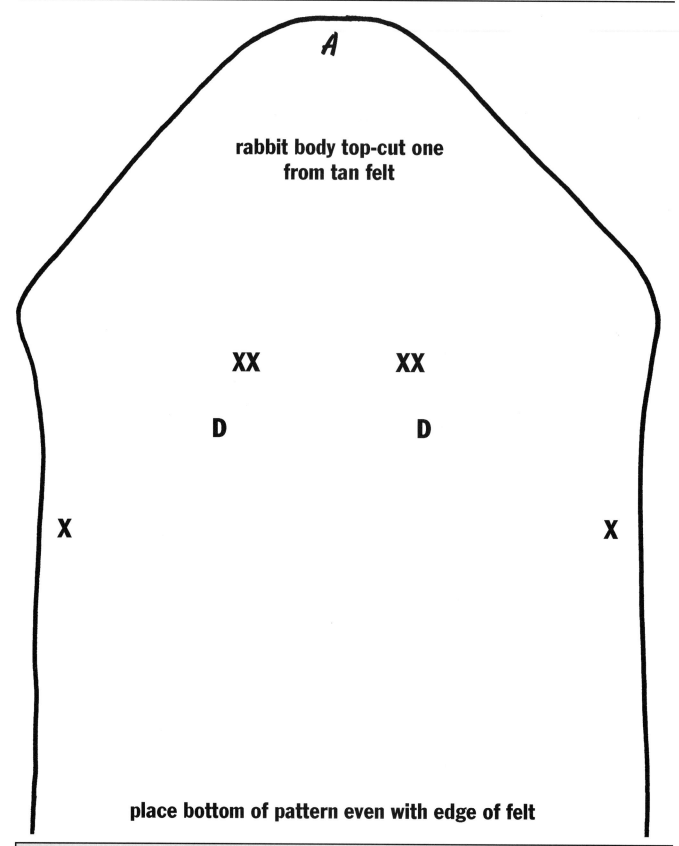

A

rabbit body top-cut one
from tan felt

XX   XX

D   D

X   X

place bottom of pattern even with edge of felt

Figure 3.19 Pattern for Jackrabbit Puppet

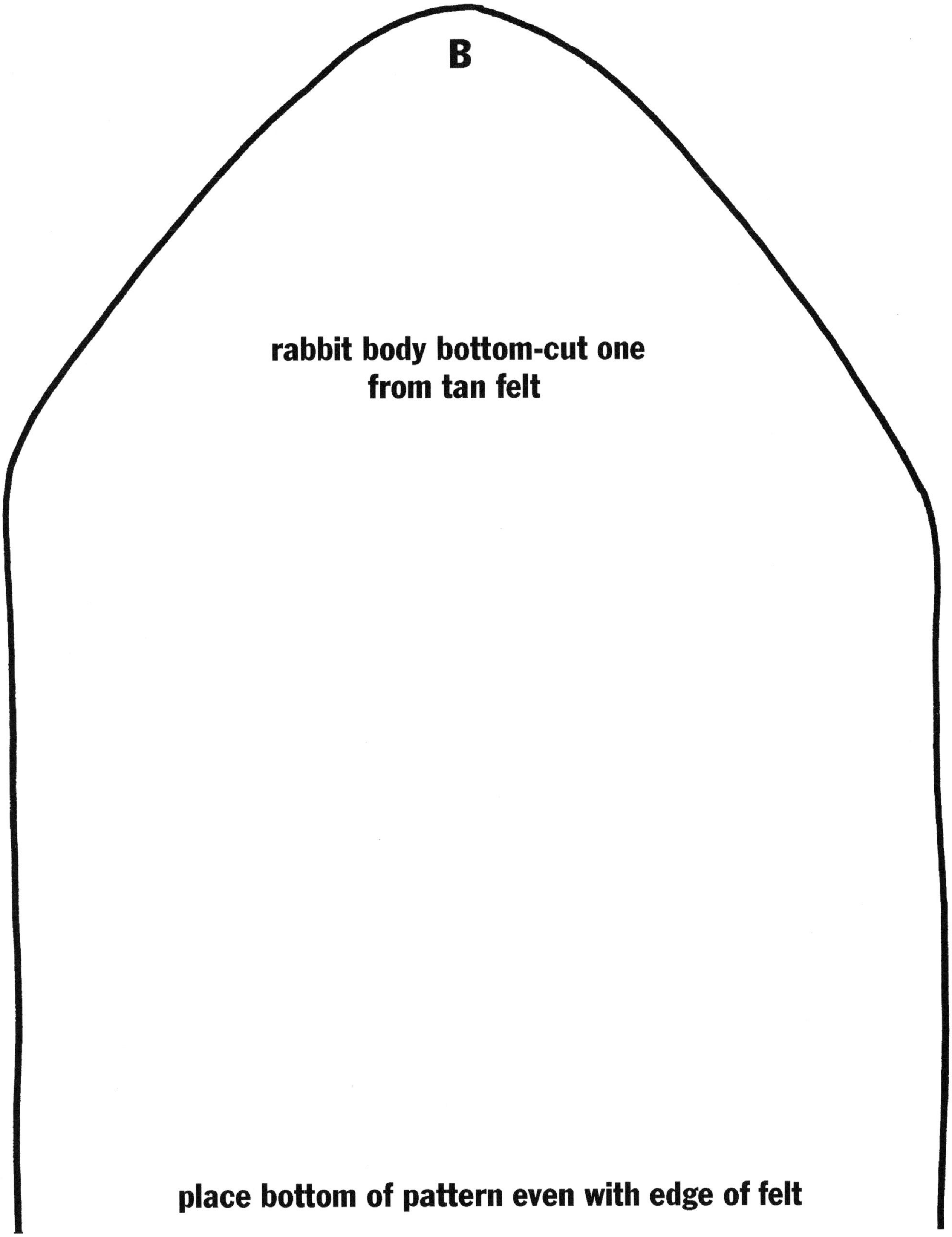

B

**rabbit body bottom-cut one
from tan felt**

place bottom of pattern even with edge of felt

Figure 3.20 Pattern for Jackrabbit Puppet

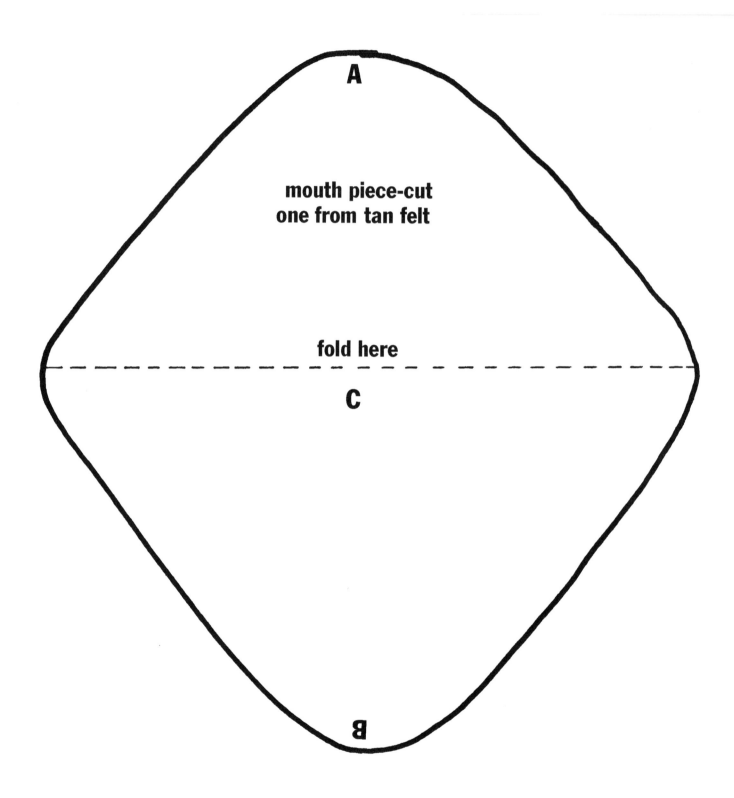

Figure 3.21 Pattern for Jackrabbit Puppet

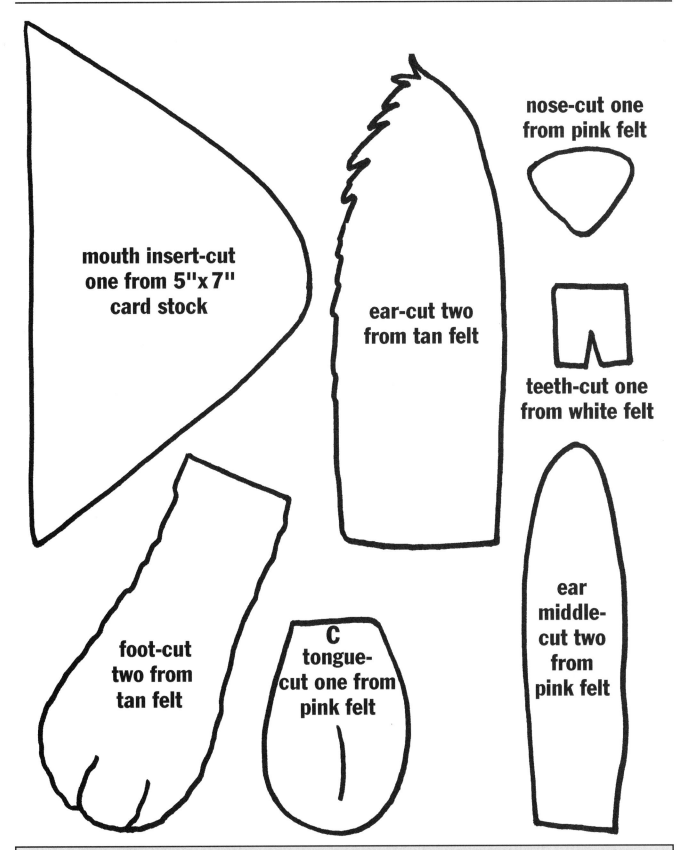

mouth insert-cut one from 5"x 7" card stock

nose-cut one from pink felt

ear-cut two from tan felt

teeth-cut one from white felt

ear middle-cut two from pink felt

foot-cut two from tan felt

C
tongue-cut one from pink felt

Figure 3.22 Pattern Pieces for Jackrabbit Puppet

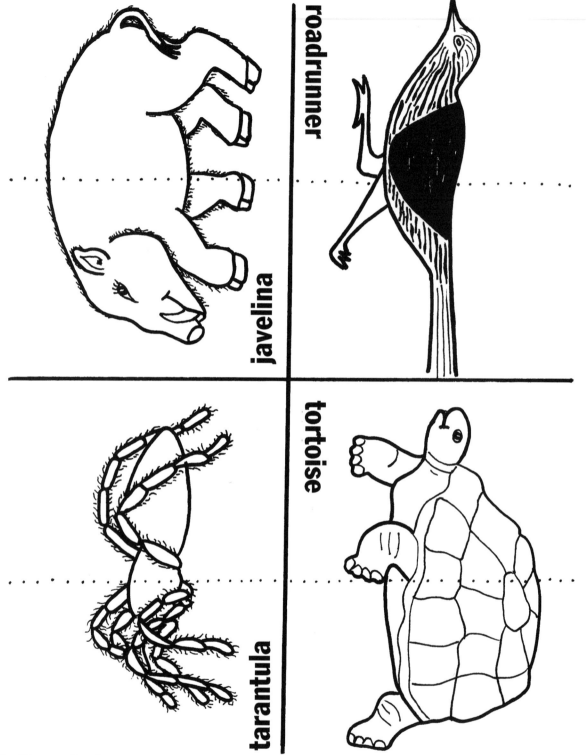

To Make Picture Cards:

1. Reproduce, color, and laminate the following pictures: tarantula, roadrunner, javelina, and tortoise.
2. Cut each picture in half, on the dotted line, as indicated.

Figure 3.23 Cards for Matching Activity

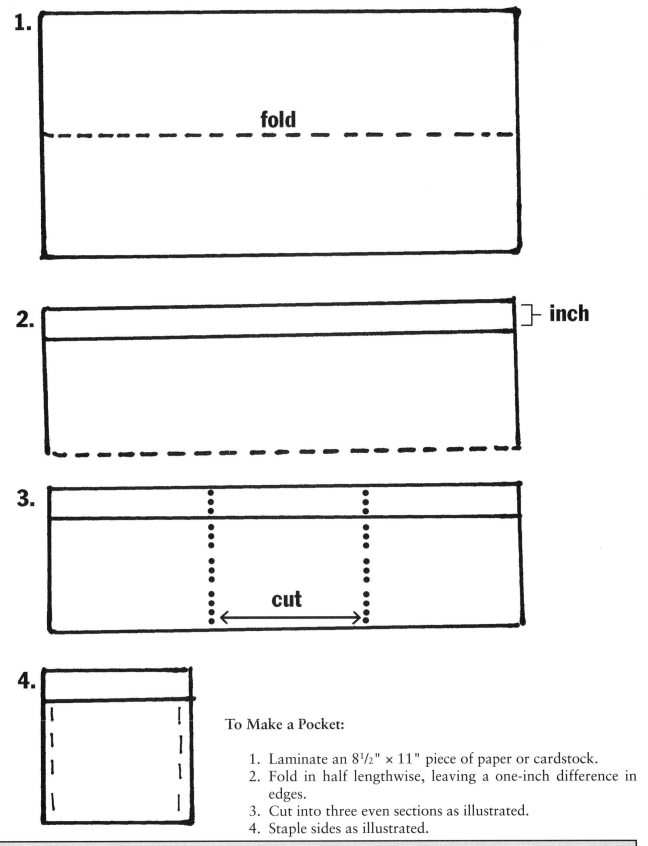

1.

fold

2.

⊐ **inch**

3.

cut

4.

To Make a Pocket:

1. Laminate an $8^{1}/_{2}$" × 11" piece of paper or cardstock.
2. Fold in half lengthwise, leaving a one-inch difference in edges.
3. Cut into three even sections as illustrated.
4. Staple sides as illustrated.

Figure 3.24 Instructions for Matching Pocket Activity

To Make as a Flannel Story:

1. Reproduce crow pattern five times.
2. Cut all patterns from black felt.
3. Enhance with felt markers.

To Make as a Magnetic Story:

1. Reproduce crow pattern five times.
2. Color in colors of your choice.
3. Laminate.
4. Cut out.
5. Attach a magnetic strip to the back of each piece.

Figure 3.25 Pattern for "Five Black and Shiny Crows"

Coloring Sheet

Shady Hat

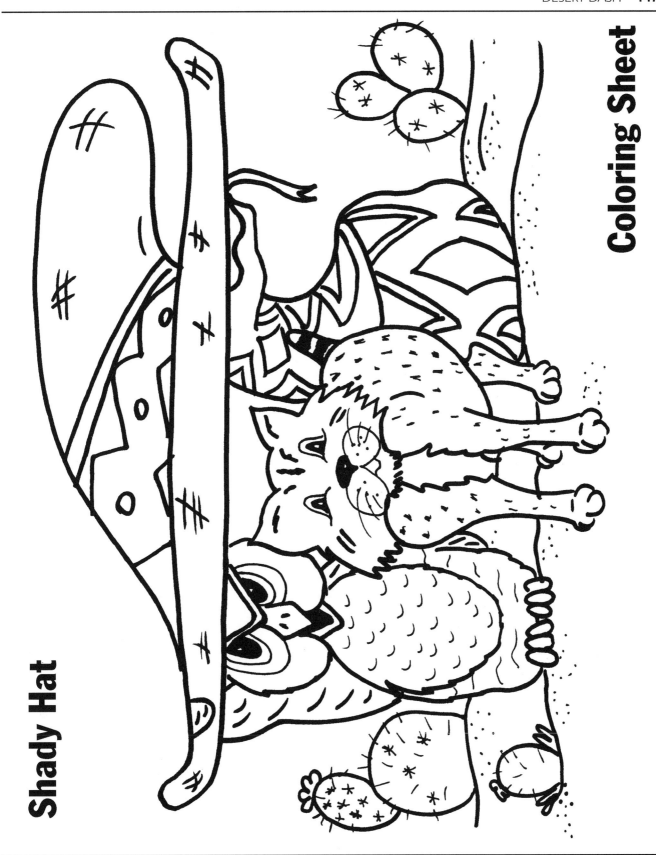

Figure 3.26 "Shady Hat" Coloring Sheet

To make finger puppets:
    1. color all coyotes and cut out
    2. measure to fit each finger and
       thumb, then tape

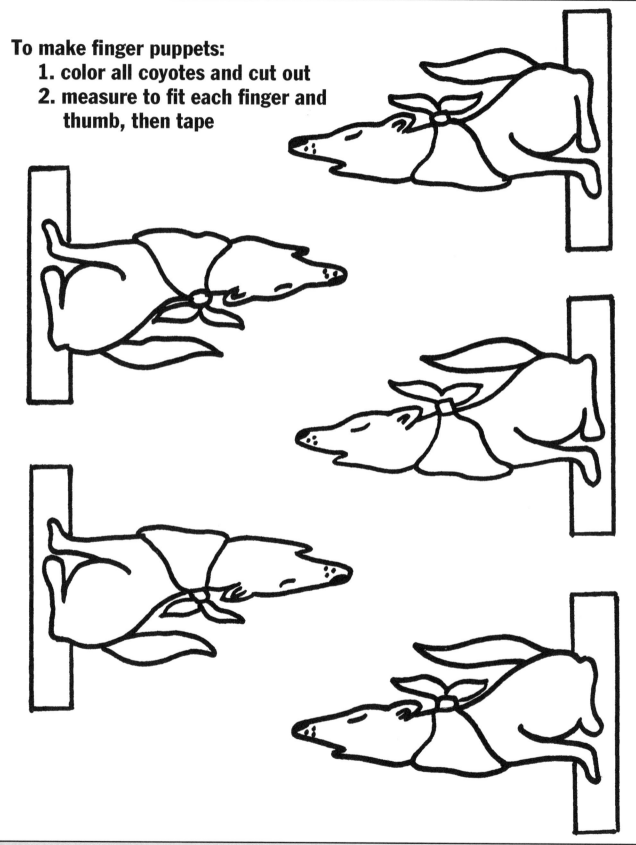

Figure 3.27 Activity Sheet for "Five Little Coyotes"

CHAPTER FOUR

Beach Party

Beach Party Outline

Share an underwater adventure with stories that kids will dive into.

The Welcome Song page 149 (*song #1 from CD*)
Read-A-Loud page 149 (*book*)
Little Hermit Crab page 150 (*magnetic story*)
The Deep Blue Sea pages 150 to 151 (*action song*)
The Sand Castle page 151 (*fingerplay*)
Goldfish pages 151 to 152 (*flannel or magnetic story*)
Gathering Seashells pages 152 to 153 (*flannel or prop story*)
Little Seashell page 153 (*fingerplay*)
Matching page 153 (*parent and child activity*)
The Stretch and Sit Song page 153 (*song #2 from CD*)
Made at the Beach pages 154 to 155 (*prop story*)
We Dove in the Ocean page 155 (*action song #10 from CD*)
Little Hermit Crab Coloring Sheet page 156 (*handout*)
Goldfish Mobile Activity Sheet page 156 (*handout*)

THE WELCOME SONG

(*play song #1 from CD to let children know you are ready to begin*)
Let's begin our storytime, see a play, and hear a rhyme. Welcome mom and daddy too, they can sit right next to you. Songs to sing and books to see, you'll have fun each week with me.

READ-A-LOUD

Choose a book related to oceans; we recommend reading Somewhere in the Ocean *by Jennifer Ward and T.J. Marsh, illustrated by Kenneth J. Spengler (Flagstaff, Ariz.: Rising Moon, 2000).*

LITTLE HERMIT CRAB

(before beginning, place the sand piece, with three shells on it, behind the plain sand piece)

Little Hermit Crab had a shell on his back and he walked down the shore with a clickety-clack.

(place smallest hermit crab on the plain sand piece)

He walked down the shore where he liked to roam with a shell on his back that he called home. Now that little hermit crab he grew and he grew, so he walked down the shore to find a shell that was new. He found a bigger shell so he traded his in and he walked down the shore with a great big grin.

(place second, larger hermit crab over the first one, hiding it)

Little Hermit Crab had a shell on his back and he walked down the shore with a clickety-clack.

(point to the hermit crab)

He walked down the shore where he liked to roam with a shell on his back that he called home. Now that little hermit crab he grew and he grew, so he walked down the shore to find a shell that was new. He found a bigger shell so he traded his in and he walked down the shore with a great big grin.

(place the largest hermit crab over both, hiding them)

Little Hermit Crab had a shell on his back and he walked down the shore with a clickety-clack.

(point to the hermit crab)

He walked down the shore where he liked to roam with a shell on his back that he called home. As the hermit crab grew, he left shells behind on the ocean shore for some lucky child to find.

(remove top plain sand piece to reveal the sand piece with three shells on it)

To make as a magnetic story: (see figures 4.1, 4.2, 4.3, 4.4, and 4.5, pages 158 to 162)

THE DEEP BLUE SEA

(sing to the tune of "The Wheels on the Bus")

(pretend to hold fishing rod over shoulder as you sing)

I'm goin' fishin' in the deep blue sea, the deep blue sea, the deep blue sea.

I'm goin' fishin' in the deep blue sea. Wanna go fishin' with me?

(beckon with hand, and then point to self)

(rock side to side as you sing)

We're ridin' in a boat in the deep blue sea, the deep blue sea, the deep blue sea.

We're ridin' in a boat in the deep blue sea. Wanna go fishin' with me?
>   (*beckon with hand, and then point to self*)
>   (*pretend to cast line as you sing*)

We're castin' our line in the deep blue sea, the deep blue sea, the deep blue sea.

We're castin' our line in the deep blue sea. Wanna go fishin' with me?
>   (*beckon with hand, and then point to self*)
>   (*using both hands, pretend to scoop up fish as you sing*)

We're bringin' home the fish in the deep blue sea, the deep blue sea, the deep blue sea.

We're bringin' home the fish in the deep blue sea. You wanna have dinner with me?
>   (*beckon with hand, and then point to self*)

THE SAND CASTLE

I built a little castle, I made it out of sand.
>   (*cup hands together and pretend you're holding something*)

I packed it very carefully to be sure that it would stand.
>   (*using both hands, pretend to pack sand*)

I stood upon the seashore, (*stand at attention*) it stood right next to me.
>   (*hold hand, away from body, waist high and palm down*)

A wave came in and knocked me down and washed it out to sea.
>   (*fall on ground*)

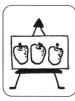

GOLDFISH

Goldfish swim by the light of day, one red and one orange, some white and gray.
>   (*place goldfish on board as colors are named*)

When diving through tunnels, shells they pass, and they nibble on the seaweed-like grass.
>   (*place tunnel, shells, and grass as each is named*)

As they glide through the water they pop every bubble, their home is safe and free from trouble.
>   (*place bubbles randomly on board*)

It's like a dance when they flick a fin. Hey! Look!

They're going around the bowl again!
>   (*place fishbowl on top of all of the pieces already on the board*)
>   (*it is important to practice the placement of the pieces; this will ensure all pieces fit within the "fishbowl"*)

To make as a flannel story: (see figures 4.6, 4.7, 4.8, and 4.9, pages 163 to 166)

To make as a magnetic story: (see figures 4.6, 4.7, 4.8, and 4.9, pages 163 to 166)

To make the fishbowl for flannel or magnetic story, you will need the following items:

- *clear laminate*
- *felt for edge of bowl (approximately 2'x3')*
- *magnetic strips (if making magnetic story)*
- *large piece of white paper (approximately 2'x3')*
- *double stick tape*
- *scissors*

1. *Place all pieces (fish, tunnel, plants, and shells) on a table.*
2. *Measure the width of the arrangement and add four to six inches.*
3. *Measure the height of the arrangement and add six to eight inches.*
4. *Using those measurements, draw a fishbowl shape on paper.*
5. *Using the paper pattern, cut fishbowl shape from felt.*
6. *Cut the center out, leaving a one-inch edge.*
7. *Using double-stick tape, tape felt fishbowl to the clear laminate and trim off excess.*
8. *Attach magnetic strips to back side of fishbowl edge for magnetic story.*

GATHERING SEASHELLS

(sing to the tune of "The Caissons Go Rolling Along")
(before you begin, place shells randomly on a flat surface; or if using as a flannel story, randomly on board)
Over here, over there, seashells lying everywhere; seashells lying all over the sand.
(point to different shells, then wave hand over the entire bunch)
Sand dollars, clamshells too, some are purple, some are blue, and they're lying all over the sand.
(point to each type of shell as it is named)
Then I pick them up and put them in my cup.
(start placing shells in cup)
Treasures for kids like you and me!
Next I look for more at the ocean's shore, gathering seashells to put in my cup!
(look around, as if looking for more shells)

To make as a flannel story: (see figure 4.10, page 167)

To make as a prop story: (see figure 4.10, page 167)

LITTLE SEASHELL

If you find a little seashell while walking on the sand,
    (*walk in place*)
bend right down and pick it up
    (*bend down and pretend to pick up shell*)
and hold it in your hand.
    (*hold hand out, palm facing up*)
When you take the seashell home,
    (*walk in place*)
just hold it your ear
    (*pretend to hold shell to ear*)
and listen very carefully, the ocean's what you'll hear!
    (*cup hand around ear*)

MATCHING

A packet, with four picture cards, cut in half, is given to each child. The child and parent work together matching the two halves to complete each picture. Make one packet for every child. Each packet will consist of four pictures and a pocket to put them in.

To make picture cards: (see figure 4.11, page 168)

To make a pocket: (see figure 4.12, page 169)

THE STRETCH AND SIT SONG

    (*play song #2 from CD*)
Let's stand up together. Now let's all touch our nose. Put our hands in the air high, bend down, and touch our toes. Let's stand up together. Now let's all touch our nose. Put our hands in the air high, bend down, and touch our toes. Now it's time to listen, so sit right on the floor. Hands are in our laps now and we are ready for more.

MADE AT THE BEACH

Here is the pie made at the beach.
> (*hold up pie every time you say the word pie*)

Here is the bucket,
> (*hold up bucket every time you say the word bucket*)

which carried the water, which goes into the pie made at the beach.

Here is the shovel,
> (*hold up the shovel every time you say the word shovel*)

which scooped the sand into the bucket, which carried the water, which goes into the pie made at the beach.

Here is the hand,
> (*hold up own hand every time you say the word hand*)

which held the shovel, which scooped the sand into the bucket, which carried the water, which goes into the pie made at the beach.

I am the kid,
> (*point to self every time you say the word kid*)

who used his hand to hold the shovel, which scooped the sand into the bucket, which carried the water, which goes into the pie made at the beach.

Here are the shells that covered the pie,
> (*hold up baggie with little shells*)

which was made by the kid, who used his hand to hold the shovel, which scooped the sand into the bucket, which carried the water, which goes into the pie made at the beach.

Pie anyone?
> (*hold up sand pie*)

To make as a prop story:

1. *Purchase or collect from home the following items: hand-digger or small shovel, plastic pail or bucket, plastic baggie filled with a variety of small seashells.*
2. *Before telling the story, place items underneath a small table or flat storytelling cart, and cover it with a tablecloth.*
3. *When telling the story, hold up each item as it is named and place on the table.*

To make sand pie:

1. *Gather the following items: one eight- or nine-inch tin pie plate, white glue, sand, variety of small shells, floral foam (enough to cover the bottom of your tin pie plate).*
2. *Cut the floral foam to fit inside the pie plate.*
3. *Taper edges to create a mounded look.*
4. *Glue floral foam into the pie plate and let dry overnight.*
5. *Spread glue evenly over the entire foam piece.*

6. *Sprinkle with sand (repeat steps 5 and 6 if necessary for complete foam coverage).*
7. *Let dry.*
8. *Glue small shells to top of pie.*

WE DOVE IN THE OCEAN

(*have children stand up and play song #10 from CD*)
We dove in the ocean and this is what we saw.
> (*make diving hands, then circle hands around eyes like a mask every time you sing "We dove in the ocean and this is what we saw"*)

A jellyfish. A jellyfish. Drifting with the tide.
> (*using hand, make a wavy motion as you move it in front of you every time you sing "drifting with the tide"*)

We dove in the ocean and this is what we saw.
A seahorse. A seahorse. Going for a ride,
> (*point your finger up, then curl finger slightly, now move hand up and down in front of you every time you sing "going for a ride"*)

drifting with the tide.
We dove in the ocean and this is what we saw.
A crab. A crab. Running to the side,
> (*hold hand with palm down, wiggle fingers and move hand to resemble a crab walking sideways every time you all sing "running to the side"*)

going for a ride, drifting with the tide.
We dove in the ocean and this is what we saw.
An octopus. An octopus. Trying hard to hide,
> (*hold hand with palm down and pretend to grab something with fingers every time you sing "trying hard to hide"*)

We dove in the ocean and this is what we saw.
An oyster. An oyster. With a pearl inside,
> (*place hands together palms touching, spread fingers, open and close hands keeping wrists together every time you sing "with a pearl inside"*)

trying hard to hide, running to the side, going for a ride, drifting with the tide.
We dove in the ocean and this is what we saw.
A shark. A shark. His mouth was open wide.
> (*place hands and arms together, touching palms and elbows; with right hand on top, hold arms out in front of you, then open and close arms keeping elbows together*)

We jumped out of the ocean his mouth was open wide!
> (*pretend to jump out of ocean*)

LITTLE HERMIT CRAB COLORING SHEET

(see figure 4.13, page 170)

GOLDFISH MOBILE ACTIVITY SHEET

(see figure 4.14, page 171)

"Beach Party" Support Materials

To Make as a Magnetic Story:

1. Reproduce patterns.
2. Color all pictures in colors of your choice.
3. Laminate.
4. Cut out.
5. Attach a magnetic strip to the back of each piece.

Figure 4.1 Pattern for Smallest Crab in "Little Hermit Crab"

Figure 4.2 Pattern for Second Crab in "Little Hermit Crab"

Figure 4.3 Pattern for Largest Crab in "Little Hermit Crab"

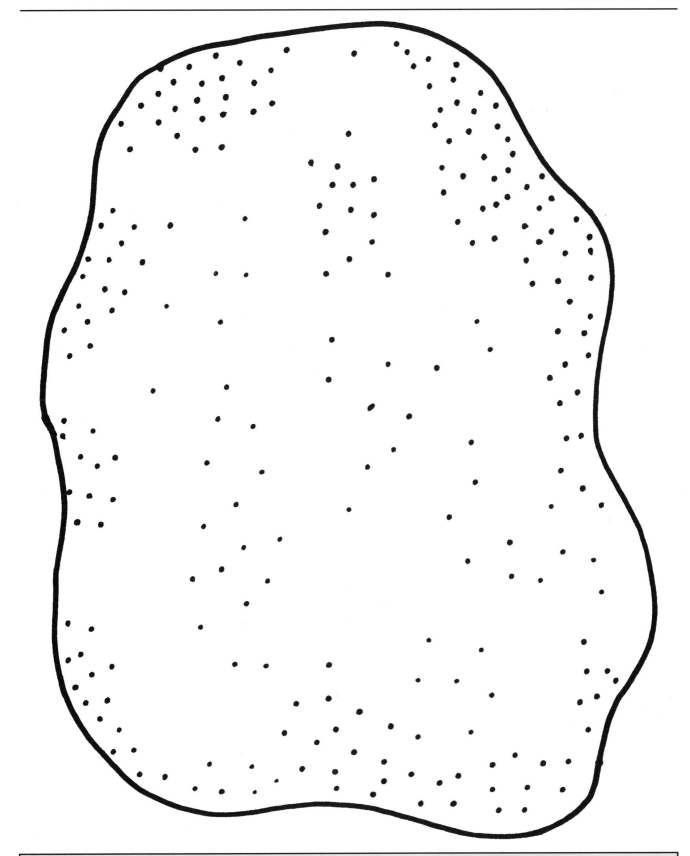

Figure 4.4 Pattern for Plain Sand Piece in "Little Hermit Crab"

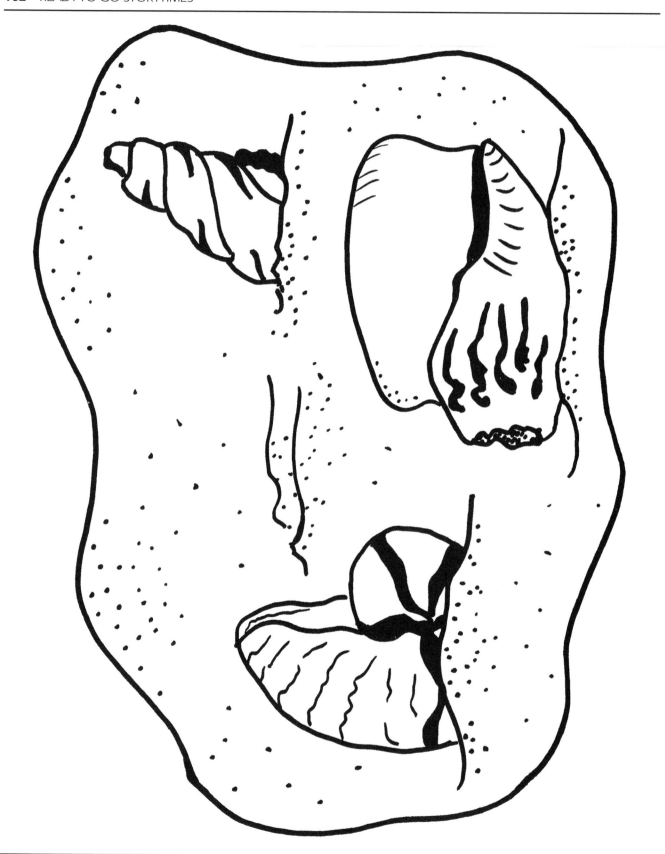

Figure 4.5 Pattern for Sand Piece with Three Shells in "Little Hermit Crab"

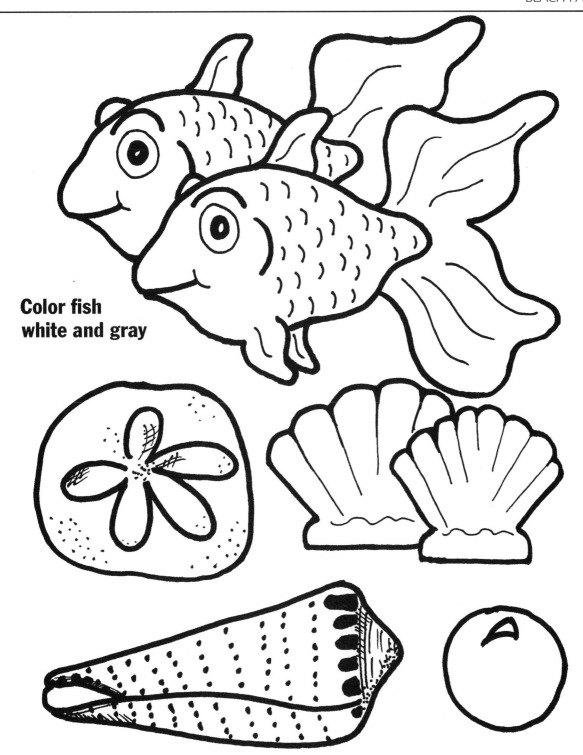

Color fish white and gray

To Make as a Flannel Story:

1. Cut all patterns from felt in colors of your choice unless otherwise indicated on pattern.
2. Enhance with felt markers.

To Make as a Magnetic Story:

1. Reproduce patterns.
2. Color all patterns in colors of your choice unless otherwise indicated on pattern.
3. Laminate.
4. Cut out.
5. Attach a magnetic strip to the back of each piece.

Figure 4.6 Patterns in "Goldfish"

color one fish red and one orange

Figure 4.7 Patterns in "Goldfish"

Figure 4.8 Patterns in "Goldfish"

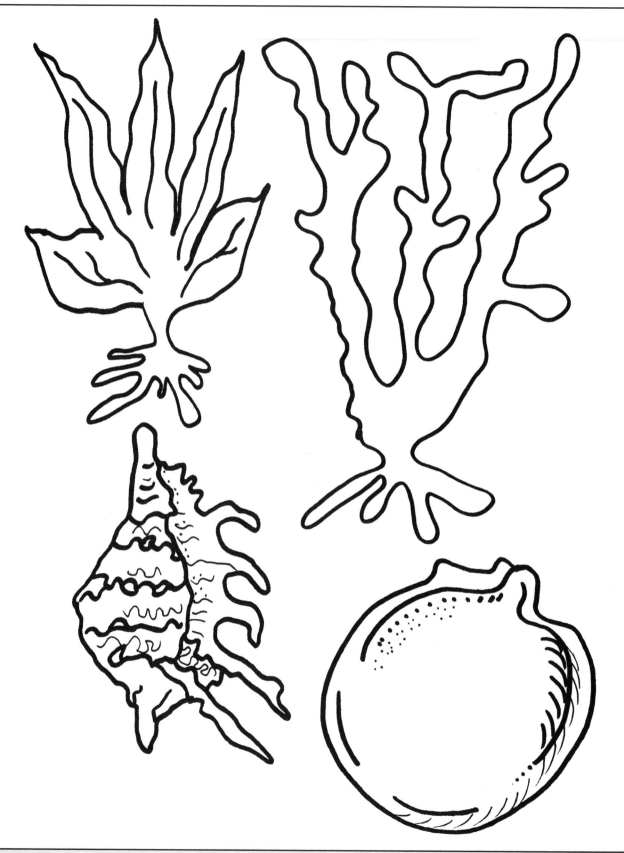

Figure 4.9 Patterns in "Goldfish"

To Make as a Flannel Story:
1. Purchase, or bring from home, one 16-ounce plastic cup or glass.
2. Cut out several of each shell pattern from felt colors of your choice; be sure to include a purple and a blue shell.
3. Enhance with markers.
4. Place the shells randomly on the flannel board.

To Make as a Prop Story:
1. Purchase, or bring from home, one 16-ounce plastic cup or glass.
2. Gather several different shells, be sure to include a blue and a purple shell (if you can't find a blue or purple shell, color shells with markers or chalk).
3. Place shells randomly on a flat surface.

Figure 4.10 Patterns in "Gathering Seashells"

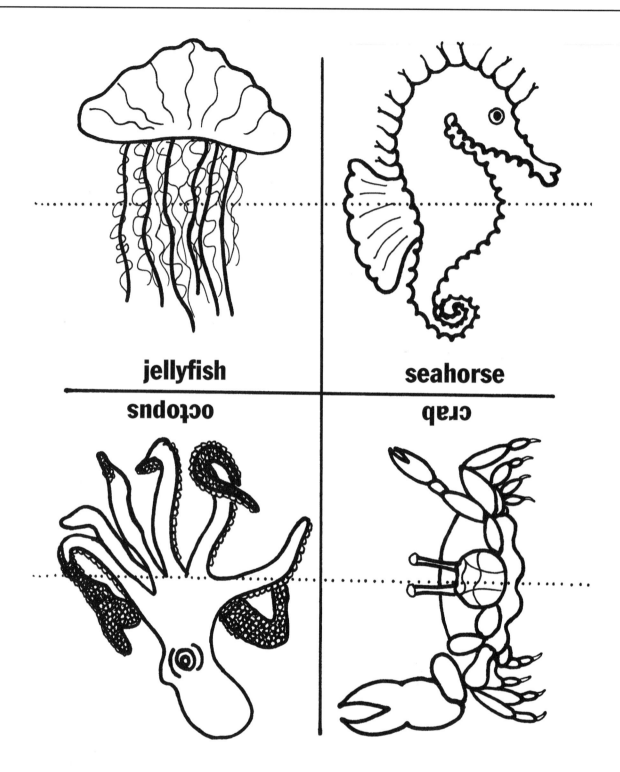

jellyfish   **seahorse**

octopus   **crab**

To Make Picture Cards:

1. Reproduce, color, and laminate the following pictures: seahorse, crab, octopus, and jellyfish.
2. Cut each picture in half on the dotted line, as indicated.

Figure 4.11 Cards for Matching Activity

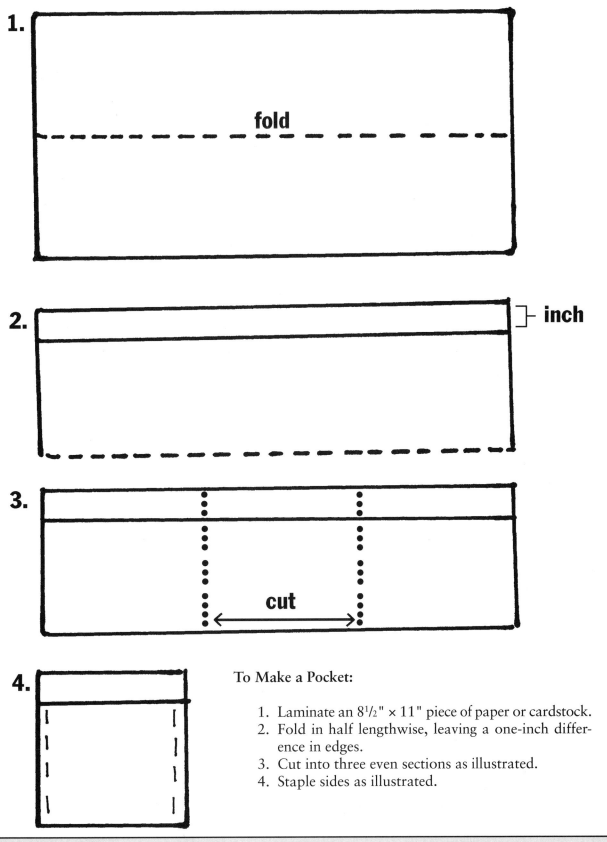

1.

fold

2. inch

3. cut

4.

To Make a Pocket:

1. Laminate an 8½" × 11" piece of paper or cardstock.
2. Fold in half lengthwise, leaving a one-inch difference in edges.
3. Cut into three even sections as illustrated.
4. Staple sides as illustrated.

Figure 4.12 Instructions for Matching Activity Pocket

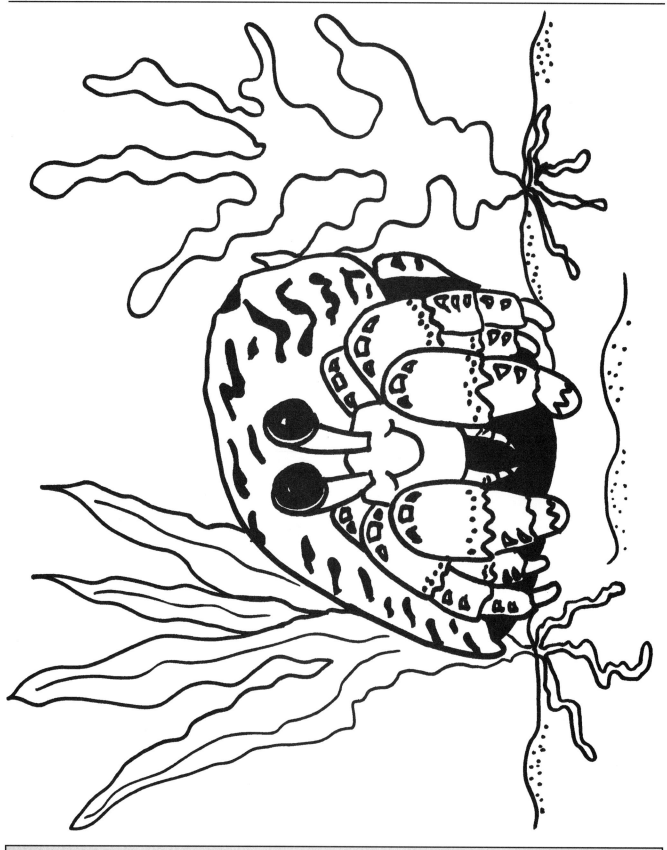

Figure 4.13 Little Hermit Crab Coloring Sheet

To make mobile:
1. **color pictures and cut out**
2. **punch hole at top of each picture and tie varying lengths of thread or fishing line through each hole**
3. **shape a wire clothes hanger into a circle, forming a fishbowl**
4. **tie pictures at varying heights within the clothes hanger**

Figure 4.14 Goldfish Mobile Activity Sheet

CHAPTER FIVE

Color Wheel

Color Wheel Outline
Share a kaleidoscope of stories to color a child's world.

The Welcome Song page 173 (*song #1 from CD*)
Read-A-Loud page 173 (*book*)
The Blue Jay pages 174 to 175 (*flannel or magnetic story*)
Five Pairs of Dirty Socks! pages 175 to 176 (*prop story*)
All Day Long page 176 (*action song*)
Wash Day page 177 (*flannel, magnetic, or prop story*)
Mom's Little Hounds pages 177 to 178 (*magnetic story, song #11 from CD*)
Matching page 178 (*parent and child activity*)
The Stretch and Sit Song page 178 (*song #2 from CD*)
I Found a Little Box pages 178 to 179 (*prop story*)
Dippin' in the Paintbox pages 179 to 180 (*action song, song #12 from CD*)
Blue Jay Coloring Sheet page 200 (*handout*)
Color Dominos Activity Sheet page 201 (*handout*)

THE WELCOME SONG

(play song #1 from CD to let children know you are ready to begin)
Let's begin our storytime, see a play, and hear a rhyme. Welcome mom and daddy too, they can sit right next to you. Songs to sing and books to see, you'll have fun each week with me.

READ-A-LOUD

Choose a book related to colors; we recommend reading Brown Bear, Brown Bear, What Do You See? *by Bill Martin, illustrated by Eric Carle (New York: Holt, Rinehart, Winston, 1983).*

THE BLUE JAY

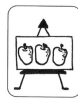

(before beginning place branches on board)
A Blue Jay and his wife built a nest of sticks and straw, grass and feathers.

(place nest on board)
When it was ready Mrs. Jay laid three beautiful eggs.

(place eggs in nest)
She was very excited about the eggs and she showed them to Mr. Jay. Then she settled herself down on the eggs in the nest to wait for her babies to hatch.

(place Mrs. Jay, with baby Jays behind her, on eggs)
Mr. Jay was worried about Mrs. Jay, because he knew she would not leave her nest to eat, while she waited for her babies to hatch. He decided to entice her with tasty tidbits from the park around their tree. Mr. Jay flew off to find something tasty, leaving Mrs. Jay singing on her nest, "Babies are the best to fill an empty nest."

(remove Mr. Jay from board)
Soon Mr. Jay returned with a piece of pink watermelon he had found on the playground.

(place Mr. Jay on board with watermelon in his beak)
He laid the piece of pink watermelon on the branch.

(place watermelon on branch)
But Mrs. Jay had a job to do; she was keeping her eggs warm. She didn't eat the piece of pink watermelon. Mr. Jay flew off to find something even tastier.

(remove Mr. Jay from board)
Mrs. Jay sat singing on her nest, "Babies are the best to fill an empty nest." Soon Mr. Jay returned with a big green lettuce leaf he had found on the park bench.

(place Mr. Jay on board with lettuce on his beak)
He laid the big green lettuce leaf on the branch.

(place lettuce on branch)
But Mrs. Jay had a job to do; she was keeping her eggs warm. She didn't eat the big green lettuce leaf. Mr. Jay flew off to find something even tastier.

(remove Mr. Jay from board)
Mrs. Jay sat singing on her nest, "Babies are the best to fill an empty nest." Soon Mr. Jay returned with a plump red strawberry he had found on the picnic table.

(place Mr. Jay on board with strawberry on his beak)
He put the plump red strawberry on the branch.

(place strawberry on branch)
But Mrs. Jay had a job to do; she was keeping her eggs warm. She didn't eat the plump red strawberry. Mr. Jay flew off to find something even tastier.

(remove Mr. Jay from board)
Mrs. Jay sat singing on her nest, "Babies are the best to fill an empty nest." This time Mr. Jay returned with a juicy purple plum he had picked from the neighbor's tree.
(place Mr. Jay on board with plum in his beak)
He laid the juicy purple plum on the branch.
(place plum on branch)
But Mrs. Jay had a job to do; she was keeping her eggs warm. She didn't eat the juicy purple plum. Mr. Jay stood on the branch looking down into the garden for something even tastier. Suddenly Mrs. Jay gave a little sigh and said, "At last!" She hopped off her nest onto the branch.
(remove Mrs. Jay and eggs from nest exposing baby Jays)
(place Mrs. Jay on branch next to food)
There in the nest were three little baby Blue Jays. Mr. Jay said, "What a beautiful family we have!" But Mrs. Jay was too busy eating, she couldn't say anything at all!

To make as a flannel story: (see figures 5.1, 5.2, 5.3, 5.4, and 5.5, pages 182 to 186)

To make as a magnetic story: (see figures 5.1, 5.2, 5.3, 5.4, and 5.5, pages 182 to 186)

FIVE PAIRS OF DIRTY SOCKS!

(can be sung to tune of "The Grand Ole Duke of York")
(place all socks, except for "favorite pair," which will be rolled, individually on a flat surface and hold small basket in arm)
Five pairs of dirty socks on my bedroom floor;
Mom washed the blue pair and then there were four!
(place two blue socks in basket)
Four pairs of dirty socks that belong to me;
Mom washed the red pair and then there were three!
(place two red socks in basket)
Three pairs of dirty socks; what's a kid to do?
Mom washed the green pair and then there were two!
(place two green socks in basket)
Two pairs of dirty socks, I wear them when I run;
Mom washed the white pair and then there was one!
(place two white socks in basket)
One pair of dirty socks rolled up in a ball;
Mom washed the last pair, my favorite pair of all!
(place rolled pair of socks in basket)

No more dirty socks, Mom washed them all today;
But wait until tomorrow, there's more on the way!
  (toss socks from basket into air)

To make as a prop story you will need to purchase or bring from home the following items: small laundry basket, approximately ten inches in diameter, one pair each blue, green, red, and white socks, one pair wild or patterned socks (this will be the "favorite" pair in the story).

ALL DAY LONG

I'll be turning that red handle all day long. Turn. Turn.
  (make fist with right hand, then make small circles, pretending to turn handle; continue this motion through entire song)
I'll be turning that red handle all day long. Turn. Turn.
I'll be turning that red handle. I'll be turning that red handle.
I'll be turning that red handle all day long. Turn. Turn.
I'll be pulling that green lever all day long. Pull. Pull.
  (with left hand pretend to pull a lever; continue both motions through entire song)
I'll be pulling that green lever all day long. Pull. Pull.
I'll be pulling that green lever. I'll be pulling that green lever.
I'll be pulling that green lever all day long. Pull. Pull.
I'll be stomping that blue pedal all day long. Stomp. Stomp.
  (stomp right foot; continue all motions through entire song)
I'll be stomping that blue pedal all day long. Stomp. Stomp.
I'll be stomping that blue pedal. I'll be stomping that blue pedal.
I'll be stomping that blue pedal all day long. Stomp. Stomp.
I'll be bumping that brown button all day long. Bump. Bump.
  (nod head pretending to "bump" button with head; continue all motions through entire song)
I'll be bumping that brown button all day long. Bump. Bump.
I'll be bumping that brown button. I'll be bumping that brown button.
I'll be bumping that brown button all day long. Bump. Bump.
I'll be turning that red handle all day long. Turn. Turn.
I'll be pulling that green lever all day long. Pull. Pull.
I'll be stomping that blue pedal and bumping that brown button.
And then I'll be a snoring all night long.
  (rest head on hands as if sleeping and snore)

WASH DAY

(before you begin place yarn across board to resemble clothesline)
One big handkerchief ready for a sneeze;
   (make a sneezing sound, then "hang" handkerchief on clothesline)
One pair of blue jeans with two patches on the knees;
   (put both hands on knees, then "hang" jeans on board under clothesline)
Three pairs of shorts drying in the sun;
   (fan face with hand, then "hang" shorts on clothesline)
Four little socks, I wear them when I run;
   (run in place, then "hang" socks on clothesline)
Five new t-shirts with colors bold and bright;
   (tug on hem of pretend shirt, then "hang" shirt on clothesline)
I love washday. It's such a pretty sight!
   (hug self and sway)

To make as a flannel story: (see figures 5.6, 5.7, and 5.8, pages 187 to 189)

To make as a magnetic story: (see figures 5.6, 5.7, and 5.8, pages 187 to 189)

To make as a prop story: (instructions on page 189; see figures 5.6, 5.7, and 5.8, pages 187 to 189)

MOM'S LITTLE HOUNDS

Said the brown little hound with a faint little growl,
   (place brown hound on board)
"How long before I learn to howl?"
   (place brown "howling" hound on board next to brown hound)
Said the black little hound with a low little moan,
   (place black hound on board)
"How long before I can chew this bone?"
   (place bone on board next to black hound)
Said the spotted little hound with a weak little bark,
   (place spotted hound on board)
"How long before I can run in the park?"
   (place tree on board next to spotted hound)
Said the mother as she licked her last little pup,
   (place mother and last hound on board)
"It won't be long 'til you're all grown up!"

To make as a magnetic story: (see figures 5.9, 5.10, 5.11, 5.12, and 5.13, pages 190 to 194)

MATCHING

A packet, consisting of a three-section pocket, each with a picture secured to the front, and nine loose picture cards, is given to each child. The child and parent work together, placing loose picture cards into the appropriate pocket. Make one packet for every child. Pictures may be stored in the middle section of the three-section pocket.

To make picture cards: (see figures 5.14, 5.15, and 5.16, pages 195 to 197), reproduce, color, and laminate the following pictures: orange, pumpkin, carrot, sun, lemon, banana, frog, leaf, and turtle.

To make a three-section pocket: (see figure 5.17, page 198)

To introduce the activity, hold up the sun and ask the children a sample question, "What color should the sun be?" The response will be yellow, place the sun into the yellow pocket section. If you phrase the question, "What color is this?" as you hold up the picture of the sun, your answer may be white!

THE STRETCH AND SIT SONG

(play song #2 from CD)
Let's stand up together. Now let's all touch our nose. Put our hands in the air high, bend down, and touch our toes. Let's stand up together. Now let's all touch our nose. Put our hands in the air high, bend down, and touch our toes. Now it's time to listen so sit right on the floor. Hands are in our laps now and we are ready for more.

I FOUND A LITTLE BOX

(before you begin place small mouse or object inside the smallest box; then place that box inside next smaller box; continue placing boxes inside each other until only one box remains)
I found a little blue box right outside my door.
(hold blue box in hands)
I opened it up and looked inside,
(take lid off blue box, look inside without revealing contents, then look surprised)
that's where I found one more!

(*take green box out of blue box, setting blue box aside*)
I'll open up the green box and take a look inside.
(*take lid off green box, look inside without revealing contents, then look surprised*)
Can you guess what color might be there, trying hard to hide?
(*pause and give children a chance to guess, then remove yellow box*)
I'll open up the yellow box and take a look inside.
(*take lid off yellow box, look inside without revealing contents, then look surprised*)
Can you guess what color might be there, trying hard to hide?
(*pause and give children a chance to guess, then remove purple box*)
I'll open up the purple box and take a look inside.
(*take lid off purple box, look inside without revealing contents, then look surprised*)
Can you guess what color might be there, trying hard to hide?
(*pause and give children a chance to guess, then remove red box*)
I'll open up the red box and take a look inside.
(*take lid off red box, look inside without revealing contents, then look surprised*)
Can you guess what color might be there, trying hard to hide?
(*pause and give children a chance to guess, then remove mouse*)
Oh look! It is a little mouse, the best surprise of all!
(*if children should guess the next color of box to be revealed, when revealing simply say, "That's right, how did you know?"*)

To make as a prop story purchase or bring from home the following: five boxes in graduating sizes and a small mouse, or other object that fits into the smallest box. Change the color order in the story if necessary. If you are unable to find colored boxes, use markers to color boxes or cover with colored paper.

DIPPIN' IN THE PAINTBOX

(*before you begin, provide each child with his/her own paper paintbrush; instruct children to hold pretend paint can in opposite hand, then play song #12 from CD*)
Dippin' in the paint box, painting in the air,
(*pretend to dip paintbrush into paint can*)
rainbow colors everywhere!
(*wave paintbrush in the air, then turn around in a circle*)
Dippin' in the red paint, giving it a fling,
(*pretend to dip paintbrush into paint can*)

now there're red flowers in the spring.
    (*flick wrist pretending to fling paint*)
Dippin' in the purple paint, painting up and down,
    (*pretend to dip paintbrush into paint can*)
now there're mountains in our town.
    (*paint up and down*)
Dippin' in the blue paint, painting way up high,
    (*pretend to dip paintbrush into paint can*)
now there's blue up in the sky!
    (*wave paintbrush in the air*)
Dippin' in the green paint, painting on the ground,
    (*pretend to dip paintbrush into paint can*)
now there's green grass all around!
    (*pretend to paint on the ground*)
Dippin' in the yellow paint, dabbing here and there,
    (*pretend to dip paintbrush into paint can*)
now there're lemons for us to share.
    (*make dabbing motion*)
Dippin' in the paint box, sure had lots of fun,
    (*pretend to dip paintbrush into paint can*)
tomorrow let's paint another one!
    (*wave paintbrush in the air, then turn around in a circle*)

To make a paintbrush: (*see figure 5.18, page 199*)

BLUE JAY COLORING SHEET

(*see figure 5.19, page 200*)

COLOR DOMINOS ACTIVITY SHEET

(*see figure 5.20, page 201*)

"Color Wheel"
Support
Materials

To Make as a Flannel Story:

1. Cut all patterns from felt colors of your choice.
2. Enhance with felt markers.

To Make as a Magnetic Story:

1. Reproduce patterns.
2. Color all patterns in colors of your choice.
3. Laminate.
4. Cut out.
5. Attach a magnetic strip to the back of each piece.

Figure 5.1 Pattern for Mrs. Jay in "The Blue Jay"

Figure 5.2 Pattern for Mr. Jay in "The Blue Jay"

Figure 5.3 Patterns for "The Blue Jay"

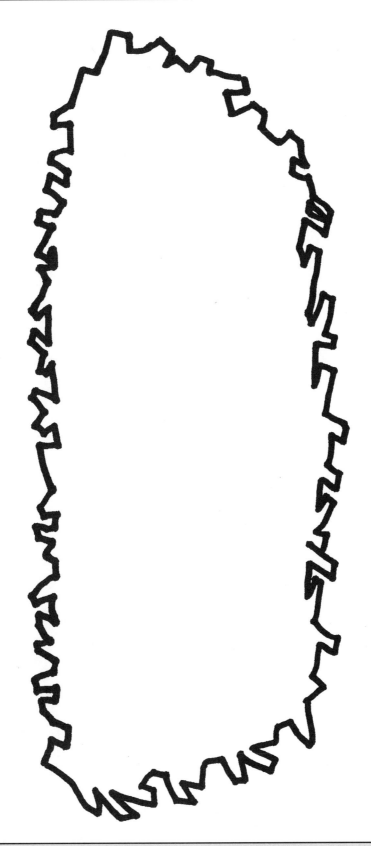

Figure 5.4 Pattern for Nest in "The Blue Jay"

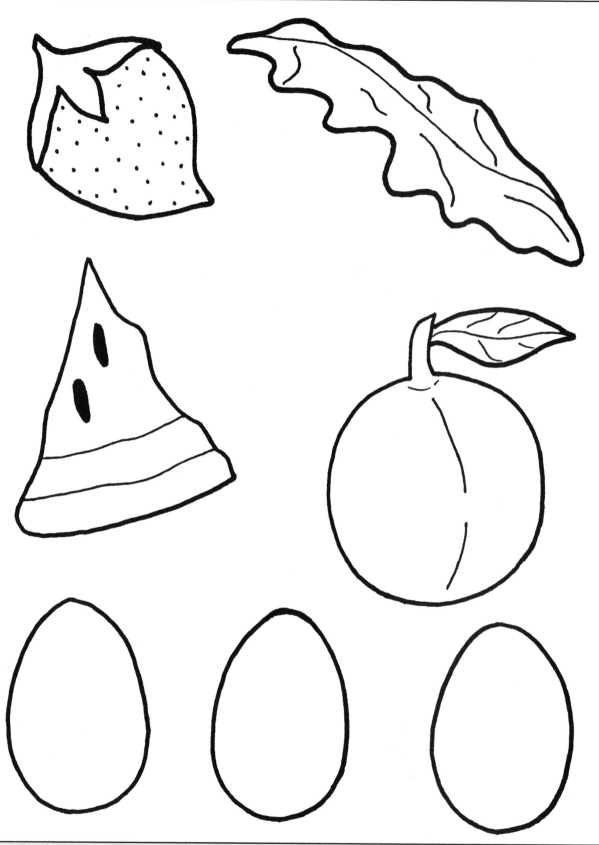

Figure 5.5 Patterns for "The Blue Jay"

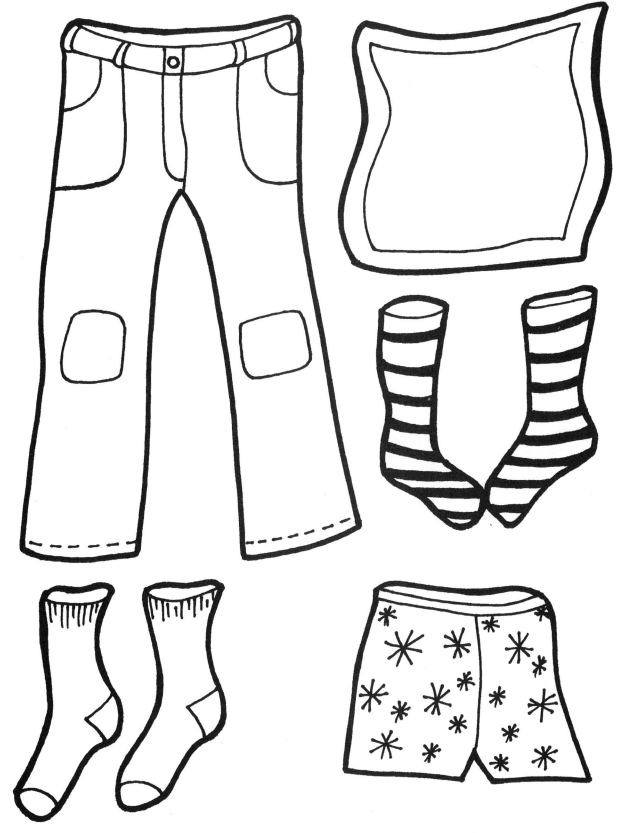

To Make as a Flannel Story:

1. Cut all patterns from felt in colors of your choice.
2. Enhance with felt markers.
3. Purchase or bring from home a 36-inch piece of yarn or rope.

Figure 5.6 Patterns for "Wash Day"

To Make as a Magnetic Story:

1. Reproduce patterns.
2. Color all patterns in colors of your choice.
3. Laminate.
4. Cut out.
5. Attach a magnetic strip to the back of each piece.
6. Purchase or bring from home a 36-inch piece of yarn or rope.

Figure 5.7 Patterns for "Wash Day"

To Make as a Prop Story:

1. Purchase or bring from home the follow-ing items: 20-foot piece of rope, 24 clothes pins, a handkerchief, jeans with a patch on each knee, three pairs of shorts, four socks, and five t-shirts (baby or children's clothing works best).
2. Stretch rope across room and secure ends.
3. Hang clothes on clothesline as you tell the story.
4. When the story is finished have children count the items of clothing.

Figure 5.8 Patterns for "Wash Day"

To Make as a Magnetic Story:

1. Reproduce patterns.
2. Color all patterns in colors of your choice, unless indicated on pattern.
3. Laminate.
4. Cut out.
5. Attach a magnetic strip to the back of each piece.

Figure 5.9 Pattern for Mom Hound in "Mom's Little Hounds"

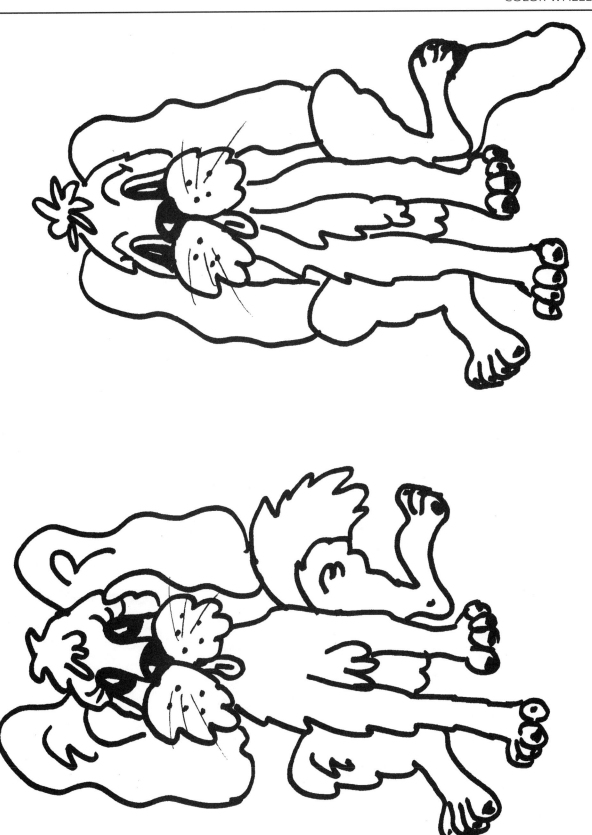

Figure 5.10 Patterns for Brown and Last Hounds in "Mom's Little Hounds"

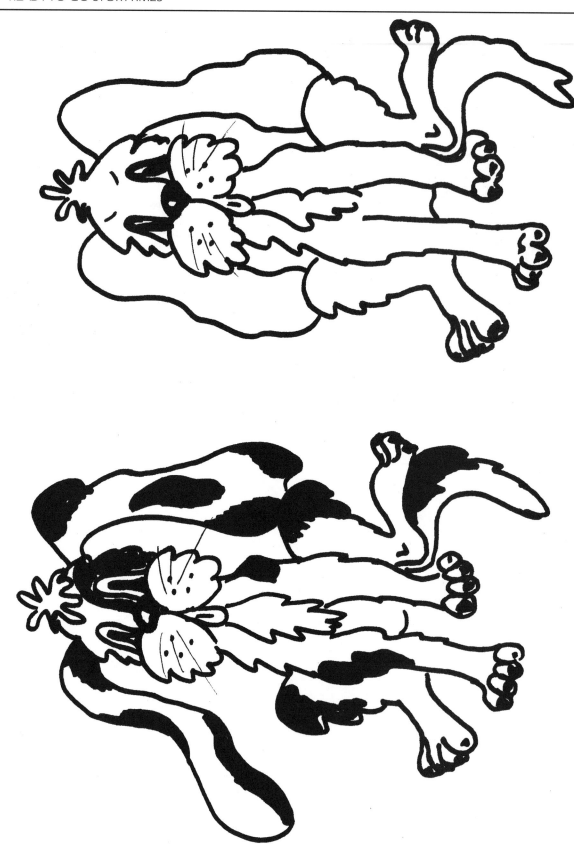

Figure 5.11 Patterns for Spotted and Black Hounds in "Mom's Little Hounds"

Figure 5.12 Pattern for Tree in "Mom's Little Hounds"

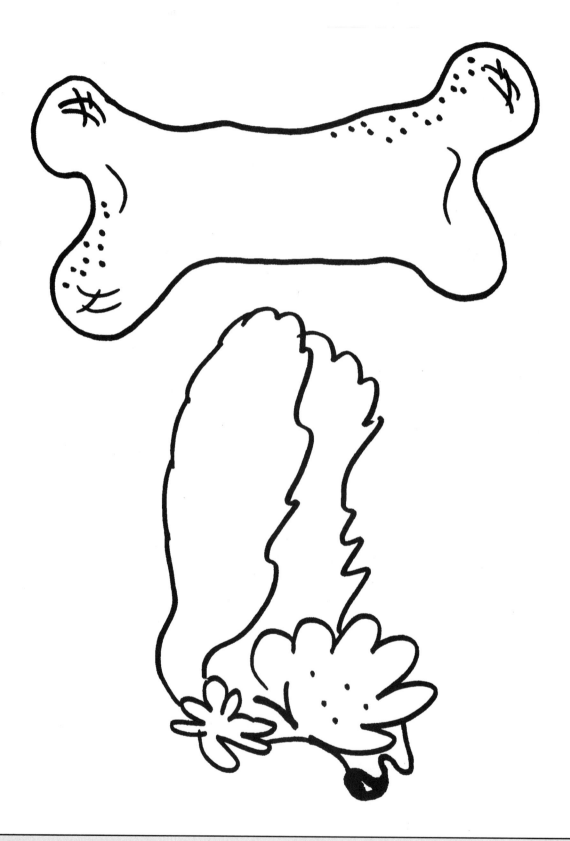

Figure 5.13 Pattern for Howling Hound and Bone in "Mom's Little Hounds"

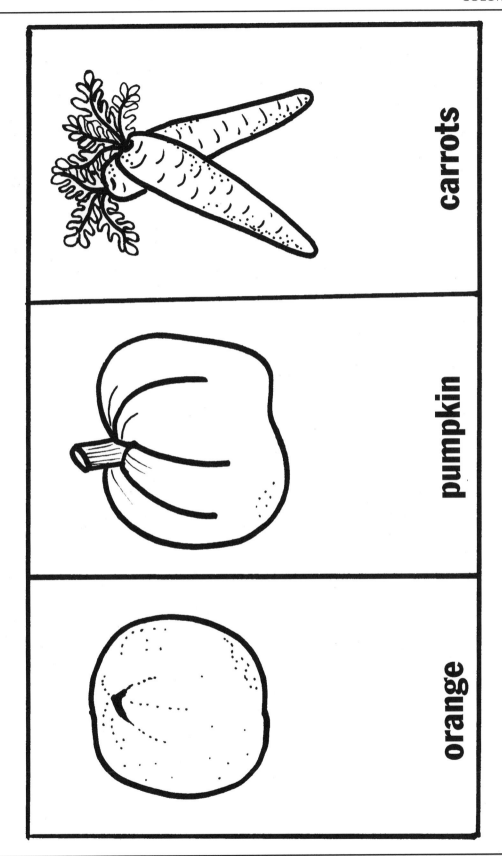

Figure 5.14 Cards for Matching Activity

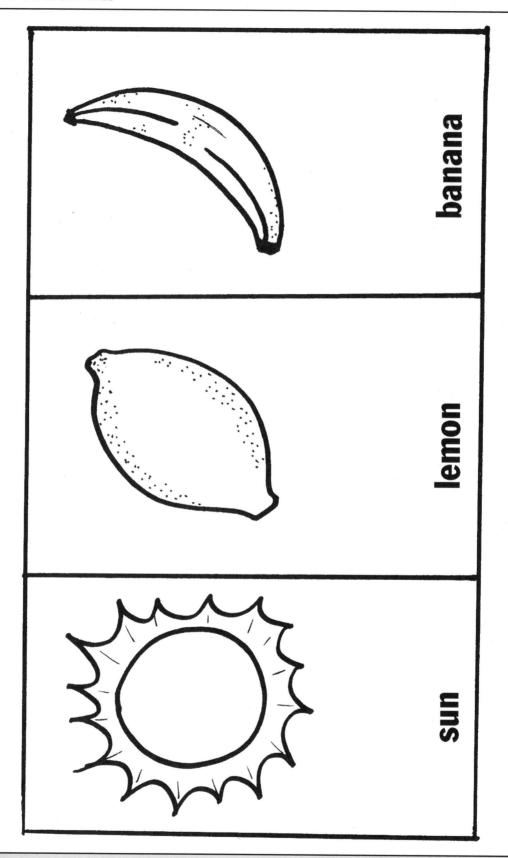

Figure 5.15 Cards for Matching Activity

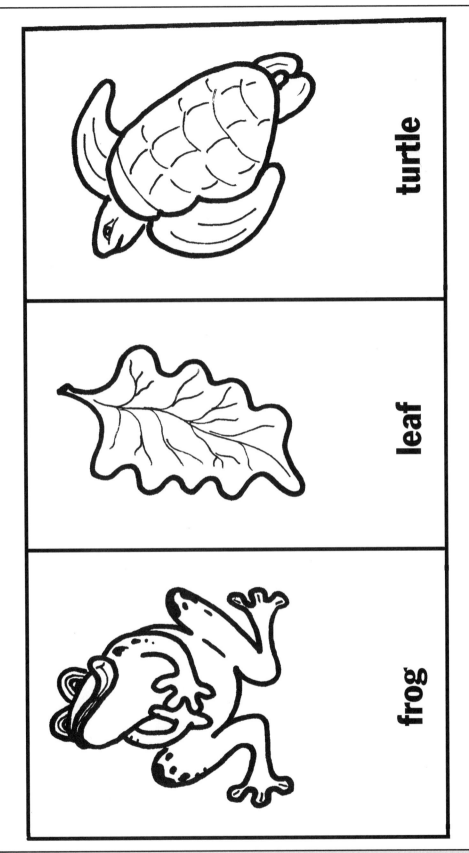

Figure 5.16 Cards for Matching Activity

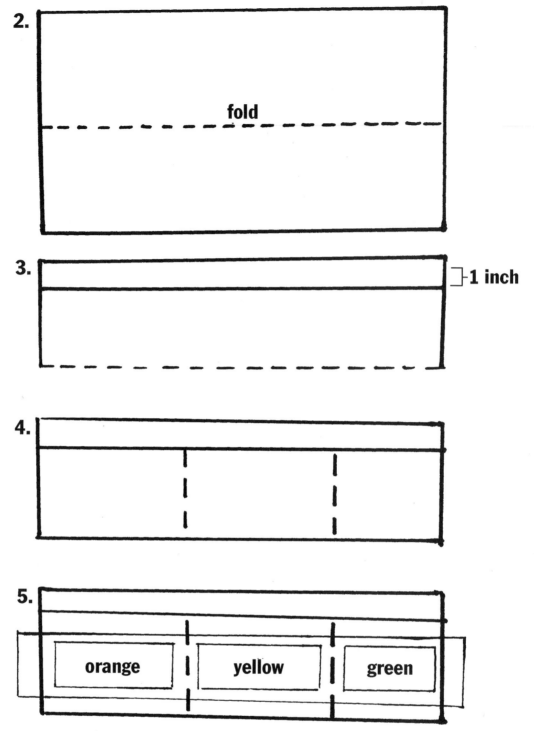

To Make a Three-section Pocket:

1. Cut 2" × 11" pieces of orange, yellow, and green paper for each three-section pocket (don't laminate).
2. Laminate an 8½" × 11" piece of paper or card stock.
3. Fold in half lengthwise, leaving a one-inch difference in edges.
4. Staple vertically 3⅝" in from each side, creating three equal sections.
5. Glue the orange paper, centered in the first section, the yellow paper centered in the second section, and the green paper centered in the third section.
6. Cut a 15-inch strip of clear three-inch-wide book tape.
7. Center the tape over the colored papers before securing. Tape should overlap each side by two inches, then press tape into place, covering pictures and wrapping the two-inch excess around each end.

Figure 5.17 Instructions for Pocket for Matching Activity

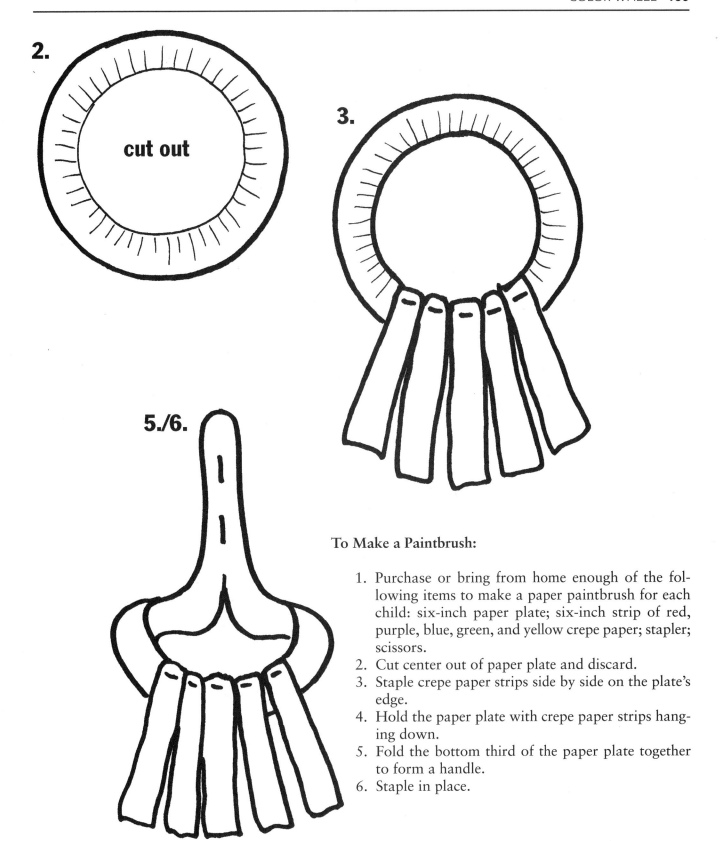

2.

cut out

3.

5./6.

To Make a Paintbrush:

1. Purchase or bring from home enough of the following items to make a paper paintbrush for each child: six-inch paper plate; six-inch strip of red, purple, blue, green, and yellow crepe paper; stapler; scissors.
2. Cut center out of paper plate and discard.
3. Staple crepe paper strips side by side on the plate's edge.
4. Hold the paper plate with crepe paper strips hanging down.
5. Fold the bottom third of the paper plate together to form a handle.
6. Staple in place.

Figure 5.18 Instructions for Paintbrush in "Dippin' in the Paintbox"

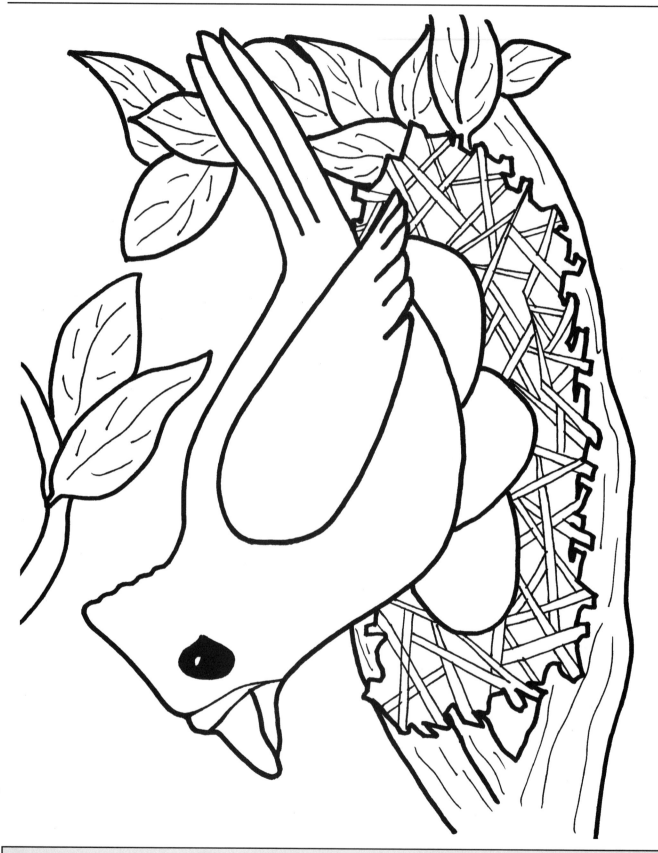

Figure 5.19 Blue Jay Coloring Sheet

To make dominos:
   1. color each square as marked
   2. cut apart on heavy lines
To play:
   1. place dominos face up
   2. match colors until all
      dominos have been used

| orange | orange |

| yellow | yellow |

| green | green |

| orange | green |

| orange | yellow |

| yellow | orange |

| yellow | green |

| green | yellow |

| green | orange |

Figure 5.20 Color Dominos Activity Sheet

CHAPTER SIX

Dressin' Up

Dressin' Up Outline
Share this closet full of stories—with kids one size fits all.

The Welcome Song page 203 (*song #1 from CD*)
Read-A-Loud page 203 (*book*)
Mom Made Me a Coat pages 204 to 205 (*flannel or prop story*)
My Overalls page 205 (*magnetic story*)
What's Inside the Pocket pages 205 to 206 (*flannel story*)
Hat, Shirt, Pants, and Shoes page 206 (*action song*)
If the Glove Fits page 206 (*prop story*)
The Clothing Chant page 207 (*action song, song #13 from CD*)
Matching page 208 (*parent and child activity*)
The Stretch and Sit Song page 208 (*song #2 from CD*)
Who's Getting Dressed? pages 208 to 209 (*prop story*)
My Big Red Boots page 209 (*action song, song #14 from CD*)
Clothesline Coloring Sheet page 231 (*handout*)
Tool Belt Activity Sheet pages 232 to 234 (*handout*)

THE WELCOME SONG

(*play song #1 from CD to let children know you are ready to begin*)
Let's begin our storytime, see a play, and hear a rhyme. Welcome mom and daddy too, they can sit right next to you. Songs to sing and books to see, you'll have fun each week with me.

READ-A-LOUD

Choose a book related to clothing; we recommend reading New Shoes, Red Shoes *by Susan Rollings (London: Orchard Books, 2000).*

MOM MADE ME A COAT

(can be sung to the tune "Turkey in the Straw")

Mom made me a coat that I wore for years, 'til I grew too tall and I cried big tears.

So Mom cut and she sewed with stitches real fine and she made a jacket from that coat of mine.

Then I wore that jacket for two more years, 'til the elbows wore thin and I cried big tears.

So Mom cut and she sewed with stitches real fine and she made a vest from that jacket of mine.

Then I wore that vest for two more years, 'til it got too tight and I cried big tears.

So Mom cut and she sewed with stitches real fine and she made a tie from that vest of mine.

Then I wore that tie for two more years, 'til I tore the end and I cried big tears.

So Mom cut and she sewed with stitches real fine and she made a patch from that tie of mine.

Then I wore that patch for two more years, 'til a hole broke through and I cried big tears.

So Mom cut and she sewed with stitches real fine and she made a button from that patch of mine.

Then I wore that button for two more years, 'til the button popped off and I cried big tears. Now Mom didn't cut or sew with stitches real fine 'cause there's nothing left of that button of mine.

Then Mom gave me a hug and she wiped my tears, as she said you'll be telling this tale for years. That was many years ago, but the story's still new; whenever I tell it to folks like you!

To make as a flannel story: (see figures 6.1, 6.2, 6.3, and 6.4, pages 211 to 214)

To make as a prop story: (instructions on page 212; see figures 6.1, 6.2, 6.3, and 6.4, pages 211 to 214)

To tell this prop story:
1. *Place the tie around your neck backwards, put coat on, put patch and button in an easy to reach place—this should all be done before the children see you.*
2. *As you sing or tell the story, remove each corresponding piece until you sing or say, "So Mom cut and she sewed with stitches real fine and she made a tie from that vest of mine," then grab the tie and pull it around to the front.*
3. *As the story proceeds, remove the tie and reveal the patch and*

then place it on your arm or leg, next remove the patch and reveal the button.

MY OVERALLS

(*before you begin, place boy wearing overalls on board*)
My overalls have five pockets to fill.
   (*place pockets on overalls, three on bib and one at each hip, counting as they are placed*)
My overalls have four buttons to close.
   (*place buttons, one on each strap, one at each hip on waistband, counting as they are placed*)
My overalls have three patches that cover holes.
   (*place one on each knee and one on middle pocket, counting as they are placed*)
My overalls have two cuffs at the bottom.
   (*place cuffs at bottom of each leg, counting as they are placed*)
My overalls have one zipper right in the middle.
   (*place zipper on front of the overalls*)
Zip, zip, I'm ready for the day!

To make as a magnetic story: (see figures 6.5, 6.6, and 6.7, pages 215 to 217)

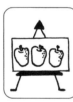

WHAT'S INSIDE THE POCKET

(*before you begin, place one item behind each pocket, on the board, in the following order: key, crayon, flashlight, and clock; pause after each question to allow children time to guess before removing pocket, revealing item*)
I have a little pocket where many things can hide.
It opens doors and starts the car.
Do you know what's inside?
   (*key*)
I have a little pocket where many things can hide.
It's used to draw in a coloring book.
Do you know what's inside?
   (*crayon*)
I have a little pocket where many things can hide.
It lights your way when it is dark.
Do you know what's inside?
   (*flashlight*)
I have a little pocket where many things can hide.
It shows you when it's time for bed.

Do you know what's inside?
  (*clock*)
We've looked in all the pockets, there's nothing left inside.
Let's play again tomorrow and see what else can hide.

To make as a flannel story: (see figures 6.8, 6.9, 6.10, 6.11, and 6.12, pages 218 to 222)

HAT, SHIRT, PANTS, AND SHOES

(*sing to the tune of "Head, Shoulders, Knees, and Toes"*)
(*point to pretend hat, shirt, pants, and shoes as you sing*)
Hat, shirt, pants, and shoes, pants and shoes, pants and shoes;
Hat, shirt, pants, and shoes; these are the clothes I like to choose.
  (*hold pretend umbrella, point from shoulders to knees, then stomp feet as you sing*)
Umbrella, raincoat, galoshes too, galoshes too, galoshes too;
Umbrella, raincoat, galoshes too; these keep me from getting soaked clear through.
  (*point to pretend sun hat, swim suit, and water fins as you sing*)
Sun hat, swimsuit, and water fins, water fins, water fins;
Sun hat, swimsuit, and water fins; these keep me cool when the heat kicks in!
  (*jump in air and click heels together*)

IF THE GLOVE FITS

A gardener wears gloves when she digs in the dirt.
  (*hold up cotton gardening gloves*)
Builders wear gloves so their hands don't get hurt.
  (*hold up leather work gloves*)
Drivers wear gloves when they're at the racetrack.
  (*hold up soft leather gloves*)
Some cooks wear gloves while preparing a snack.
  (*hold up plastic serving gloves*)
Boxers wear gloves when they're in the ring.
  (*hold up boxing gloves*)
Travelers wear gloves to visit a king.
  (*hold up "fancy" gloves, silk or lace*)
Most gloves have fingers
  (*hold up wool gloves*)
but mittens have none,
  (*hold up mittens*)
and wearing these rubber gloves isn't much fun.

(*hold up rubber gloves and toilet brush or plunger*)
Plain gloves here and fancy gloves there,
    (*select gloves of your choice and hold up*)
one thing's for certain, they come in a pair!

To make as a prop story, purchase or bring from home the following items: cotton gardening gloves, work gloves, soft leather gloves, plastic serving gloves, boxing gloves, fancy gloves (silk or lace), wool gloves, mittens, rubber gloves, toilet brush or plunger.

THE CLOTHING CHANT

    (*play song #13 from CD*)
Button, zip, or snap it,
    (*pretend to button shirt, pretend to zip up shirt, then snap fingers*)
that's what you've got to do.
    (*chastise with finger*)
Just button, zip, or snap it,
    (*pretend to button shirt, pretend to zip up shirt, then snap finger*)
to close your clothes on you.
    (*fold arms across chest, then uncross arms and point finger*)
Oh, button, zip, or snap it,
    (*pretend to button shirt, pretend to zip up shirt, then snap fingers*)
that's not the only way.
    (*hold up index finger and shake it from side to side*)
There's hook and eye, and learning to tie
    (*hook both pointer fingers together, then pretend to tie a bow*)
to save for another day.
    (*make hitchhike motion*)
Button, zip, or snap it,
    (*pretend to button shirt, pretend to zip up shirt, then snap fingers*)
that's what you've got to do.
    (*chastise with finger*)
Just button, zip, or snap it,
    (*pretend to button shirt, pretend to zip up shirt, then snap fingers*)
to close your clothes on you.
    (*fold arms across chest, then uncross arms and point finger*)

MATCHING

A packet, consisting of a three-section pocket, each with a picture secured to the front, and nine loose picture cards, is given to each child. The child and parent work together, placing loose picture cards into the appropriate pocket. Make one packet for every child. Pictures may be stored in the middle section of the three-section pocket.

To make picture cards: (see figures 6.13, 6.14, and 6.15, pages 223 to 225) reproduce, color, and laminate the following pictures: glasses, cap, hat, ring, watch, mittens, flip-flops, socks, and tennis shoes.

To make a three-section pocket: (see figures 6.16 and 6.17, pages 226 and 227)

To introduce the activity, hold up the watch card and ask the children a sample question: "Do you wear a watch on your head?" The response will be no, then ask, "Do you wear a watch on your foot?" The response will again be no. Then ask, "Do your wear a watch on your hand?" When the children answer yes, place the watch card in the pocket section with the picture of the hand on it.

THE STRETCH AND SIT SONG

(play song #2 from CD)
Let's stand up together. Now let's all touch our nose. Put our hands in the air high, bend down, and touch our toes. Let's stand up together. Now let's all touch our nose. Put our hands in the air high, bend down, and touch our toes. Now it's time to listen so sit right on the floor. Hands are in our laps now and we are ready for more.

WHO'S GETTING DRESSED?

(before you begin remove your shoes)
On my feet are two big shoes.
(put boots on your feet)
Did you hear the news? I've got two big shoes!
On my hips are tools for me.
(put tool belt around your waist)
Just look and see; tools for me!
On my hands are gloves of leather.
(put gloves on your hands)
Light as a feather; these gloves of leather!

On my head is a good hard hat.
    (*place hat on your head*)
Imagine that; a good hard hat!
For my job this is how I dress.
    (*move hands quickly from hat to boots*)
I'm a construction worker; did you guess?

To make as a prop story, purchase or collect from home the following items: pair of boots that will fit your feet, tool belt (real or paper from pattern), pair of leather gloves, hard hat (real or plastic).

To make tool belt: (see figures 6.18, 6.19, and 6.20, pages 228 to 230)

MY BIG RED BOOTS

    (*have children stand up, then play song #14 from CD*)
I wear my coat and hood; in the rain it's really good.
    (*hug self*)
But, in my big red boots I stomp my feet.
    (*stomp feet three times*)
I wear my tie and vest when I want to look my best.
    (*pretend to place fingers in lapels*)
But, in my big red boots I stomp my feet.
    (*stomp feet three times*)
I wear my holey sweater and I love it 'cause it's better.
    (*hug self*)
But in my big red boots I stomp my feet.
    (*stomp feet three times*)

CLOTHESLINE COLORING SHEET

(*see figure 6.21, page 231*)

TOOL BELT ACTIVITY SHEETS

(*see figures 6.22, 6.23, and 6.24, pages 232 to 234*)

"Dressin' Up" Support Materials

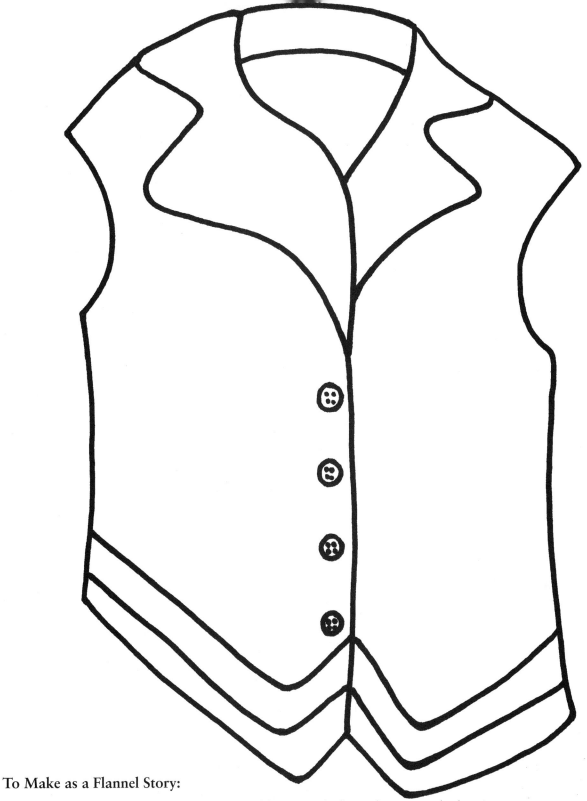

To Make as a Flannel Story:

1. Cut all patterns from bright or wild material (flannel type works best).
2. Place pieces on board starting with the button, next place the patch on top of the button (hiding it from sight), next the tie (hiding the patch), next the vest (hiding the tie), now place the bottom of coat half-way up the vest, then put the sleeves in place.
3. As you sing or tell the story, remove flannel pieces to correspond with each verse as you sing or say, "so Mom cut and she sewed with stitches real fine and she made a jacket from that coat of mine," remove the bottom piece of the jacket; continue removing pieces as the story proceeds, until nothing is left.

Figure 6.1 Pattern for "Mom Made Me a Coat"

To Make as a Prop Story:

1. Buy a bright or wild colored coat with matching lining.
2. Remove sleeves and carefully cut away as much lining as possible (this will be used to create a tie, patch, and button).
3. Cut the coat at the waist and hem edge.
4. Hem the edge of the piece just cut from the coat (this will be the removable bottom portion of the coat).
5. Attach a small piece of Velcro to the waist of the coat and the top edge of the newly created bottom section of the coat.
6. Attach Velcro to the coat's arms and armholes.
7. Sew a simple tie and patch.
8. Cover a small round piece of cardboard to create a button.

Figure 6.2 Pattern for "Mom Made Me a Coat"

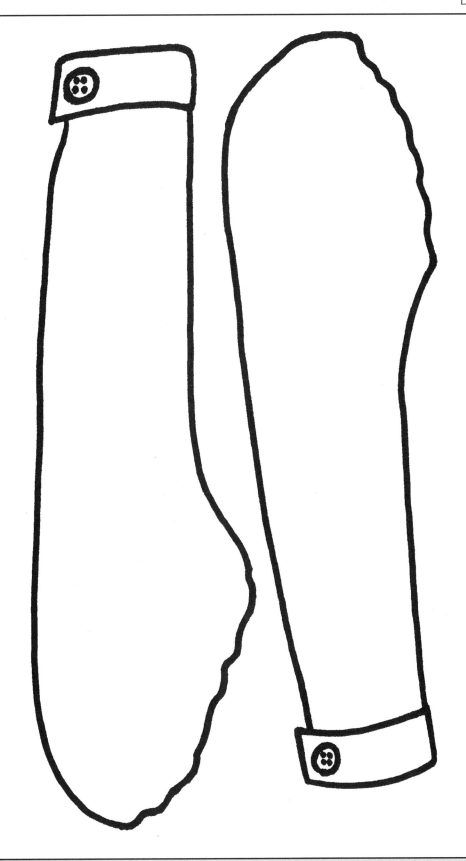

Figure 6.3 Pattern for "Mom Made Me a Coat"

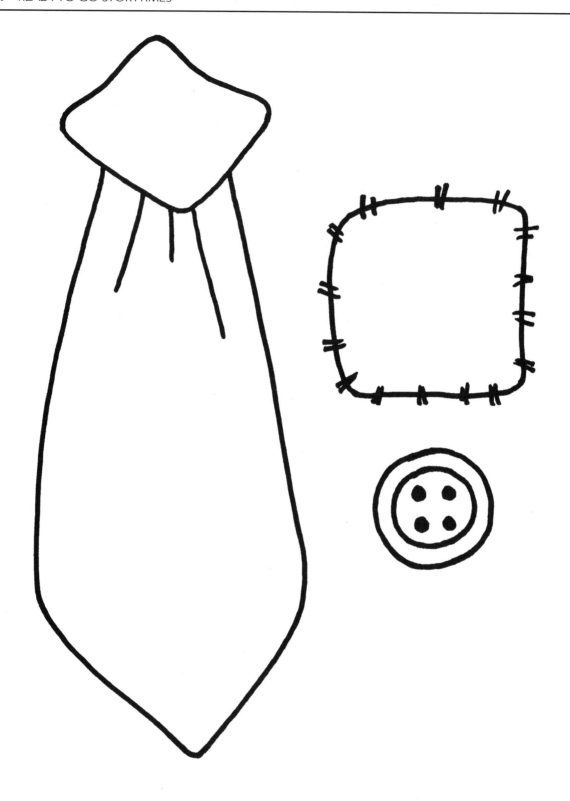

Figure 6.4 Patterns for "Mom Made Me a Coat"

To Make as a Magnetic Story:

1. Reproduce patterns.
2. Color all patterns in colors of your choice.
3. Laminate.
4. Cut out.
5. Attach a magnetic strip to the back of each piece.

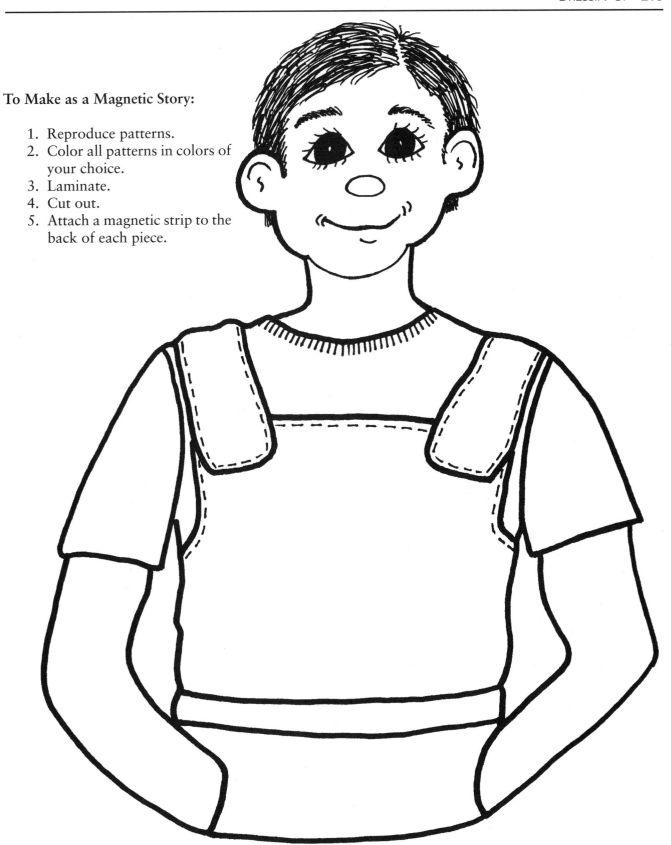

Figure 6.5 Pattern for "My Overalls"

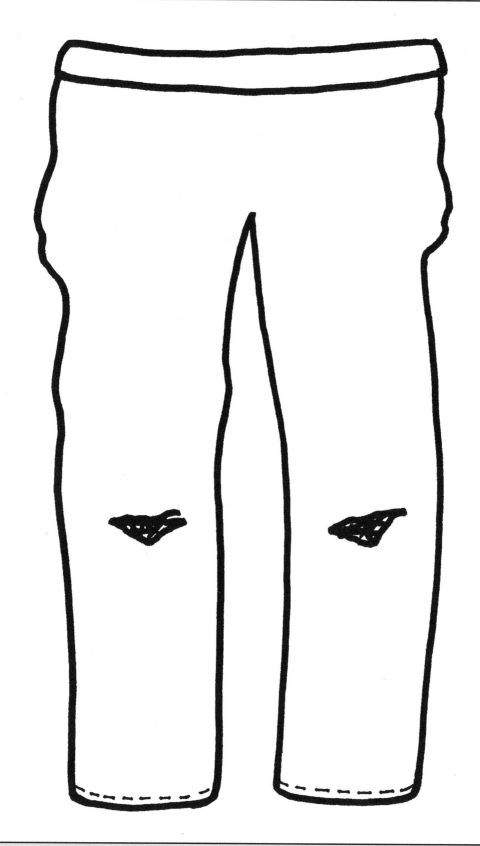

Figure 6.6 Pattern for "My Overalls"

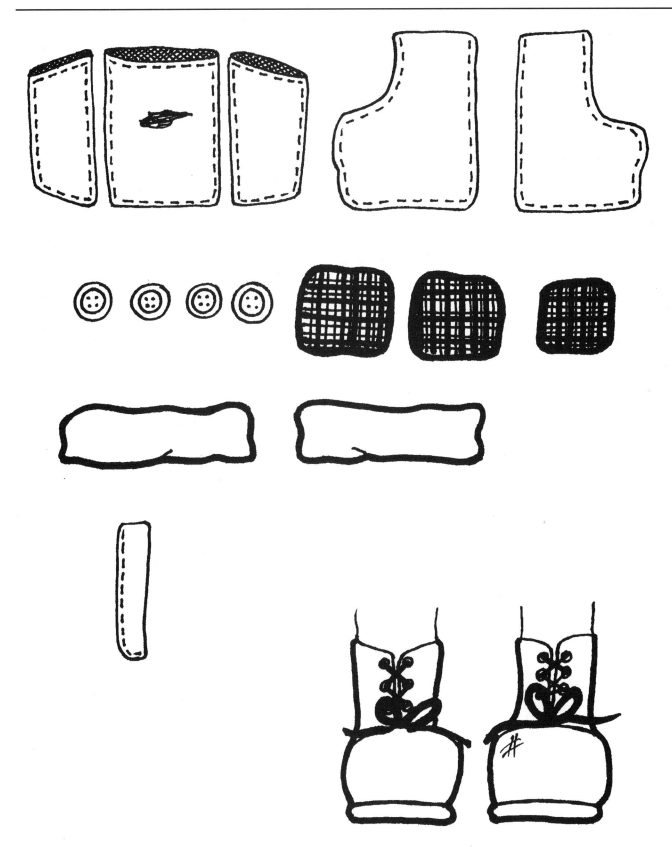

Figure 6.7 Patterns for "My Overalls"

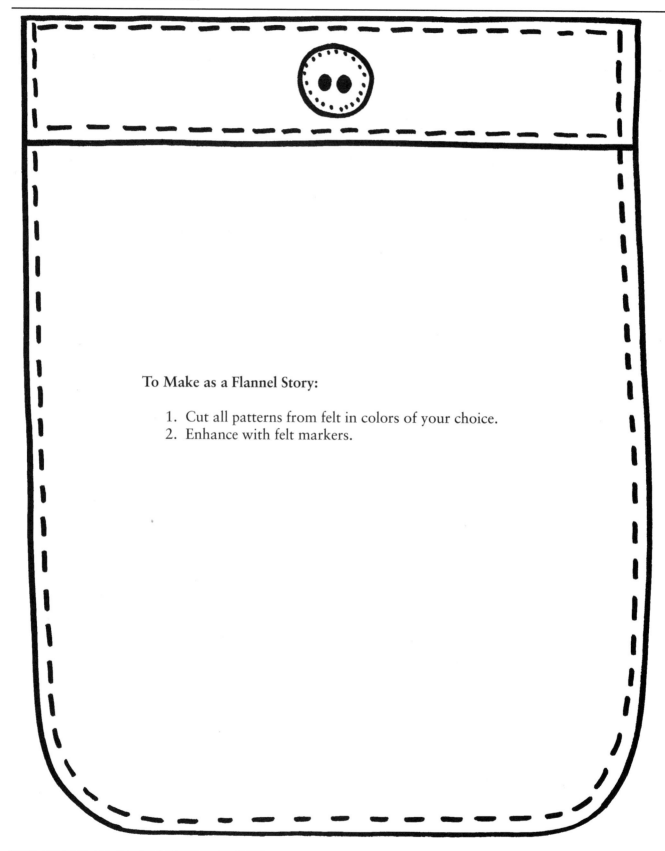

To Make as a Flannel Story:

1. Cut all patterns from felt in colors of your choice.
2. Enhance with felt markers.

Figure 6.8 Pattern for "What's Inside the Pocket"

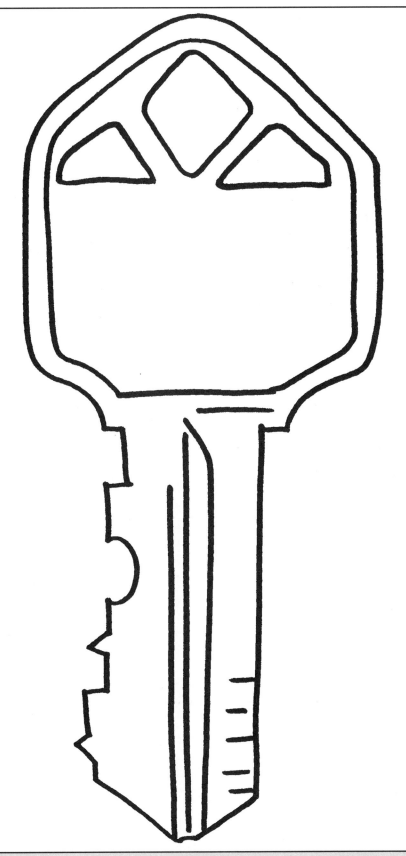

Figure 6.9 Pattern for "What's Inside the Pocket"

Figure 6.10 Pattern for "What's Inside the Pocket"

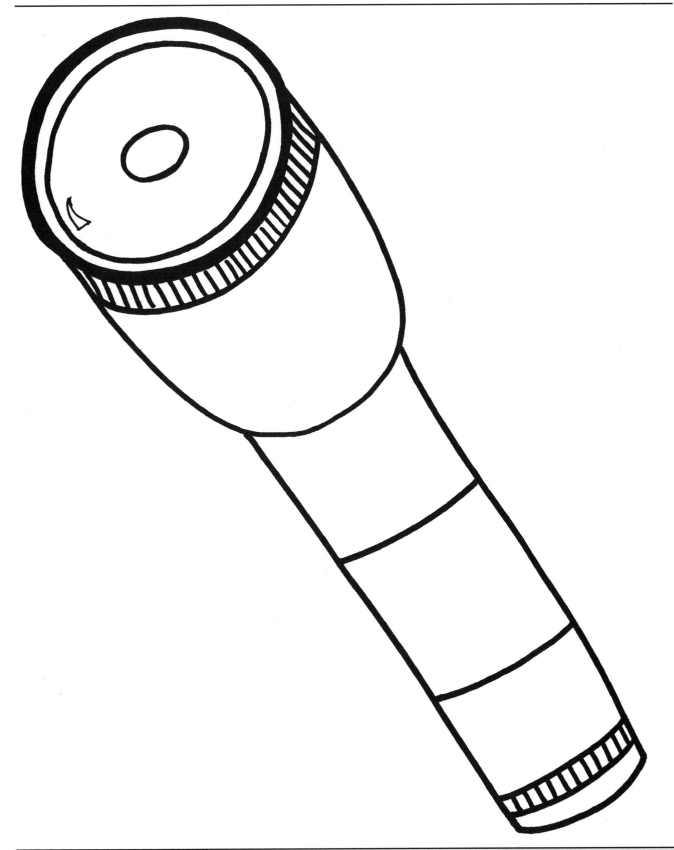

Figure 6.11 Pattern for "What's Inside the Pocket"

Figure 6.12 Pattern for "What's Inside the Pocket"

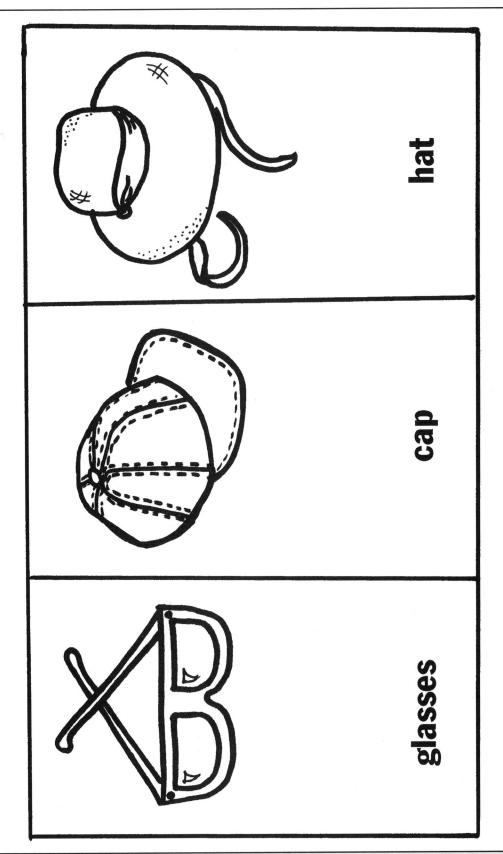

Figure 6.13 Cards for Matching Activity

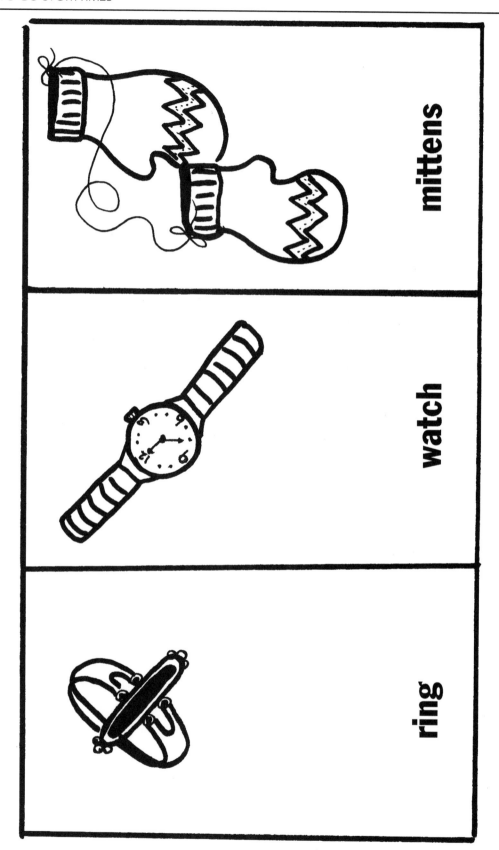

Figure 6.14 Cards for Matching Activity

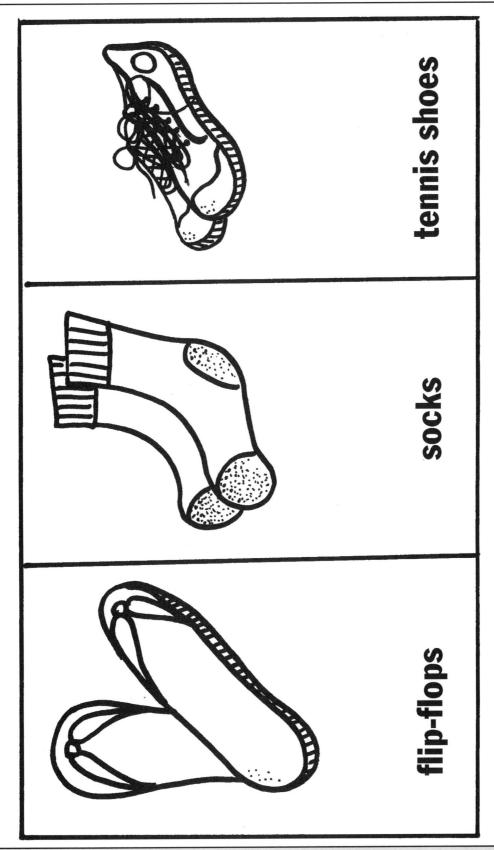

tennis shoes

socks

flip-flops

Figure 6.15 Cards for Matching Activity

1.

To Make a Three-Section Pocket:

1. Reproduce and color (don't laminate) the following pictures: head, hand, and foot.
2. Laminate an $8\frac{1}{2}$"x11" piece of paper or card stock.
3. Fold in half lengthwise, leaving a one-inch difference in edges.
4. Staple vertically $3\frac{5}{8}$" in from each side, creating three equal sections.
5. Glue the head picture, centered in the first section, the hand picture centered in the second section, and the foot picture centered in the third section.
6. Cut a 15-inch strip of clear three-inch-wide book tape.
7. Center the tape over pictures before securing, tape should overlap each side by two inches, then press tape into place, covering pictures and wrapping the two-inch excess around each end.

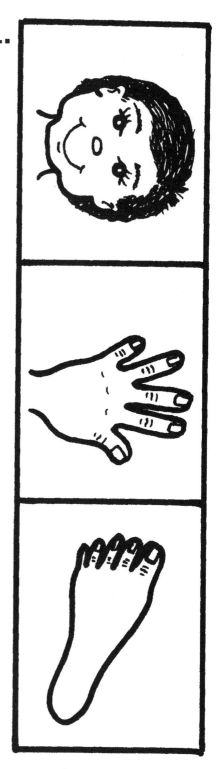

Figure 6.16 Instructions and Patterns for Matching Activity

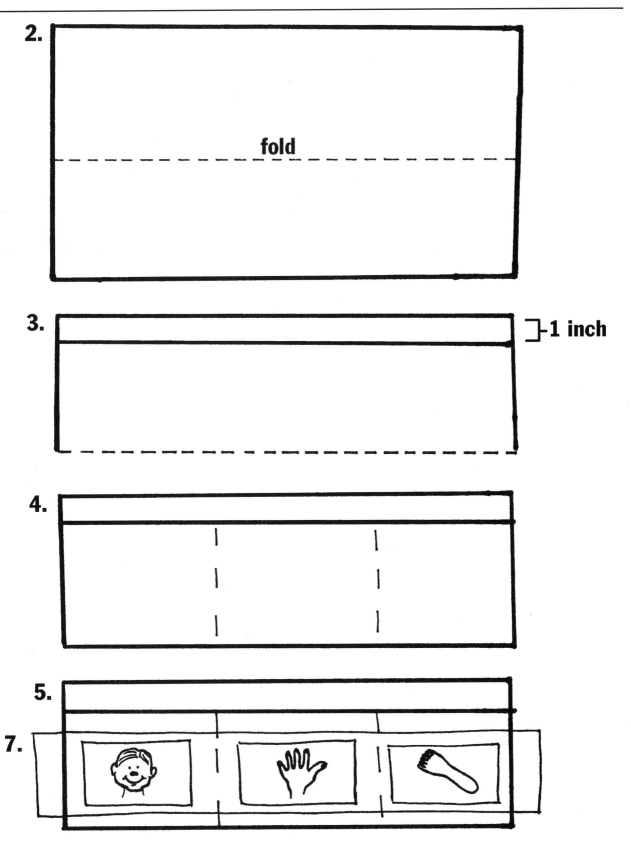

Figure 6.17 Instructions for Matching Activity Pocket

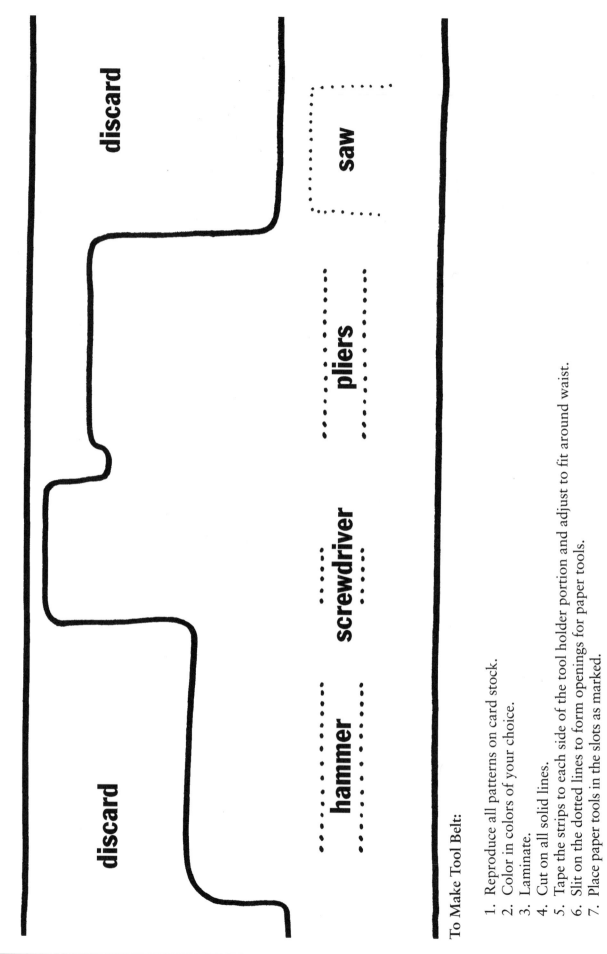

To Make Tool Belt:

1. Reproduce all patterns on card stock.
2. Color in colors of your choice.
3. Laminate.
4. Cut on all solid lines.
5. Tape the strips to each side of the tool holder portion and adjust to fit around waist.
6. Slit on the dotted lines to form openings for paper tools.
7. Place paper tools in the slots as marked.

Figure 6.18 Toolbelt Patterns for "Who's Getting Dressed?"

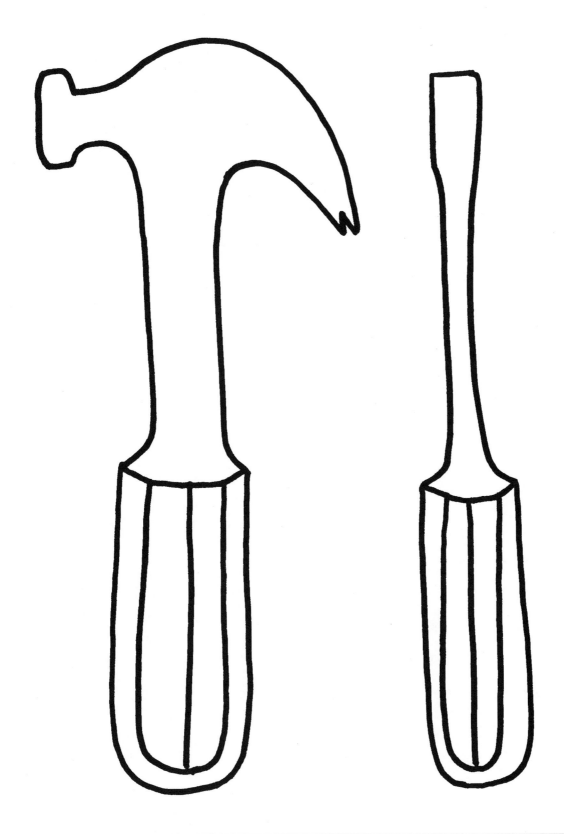

Figure 6.19 Toolbelt Patterns for "Who's Getting Dressed?"

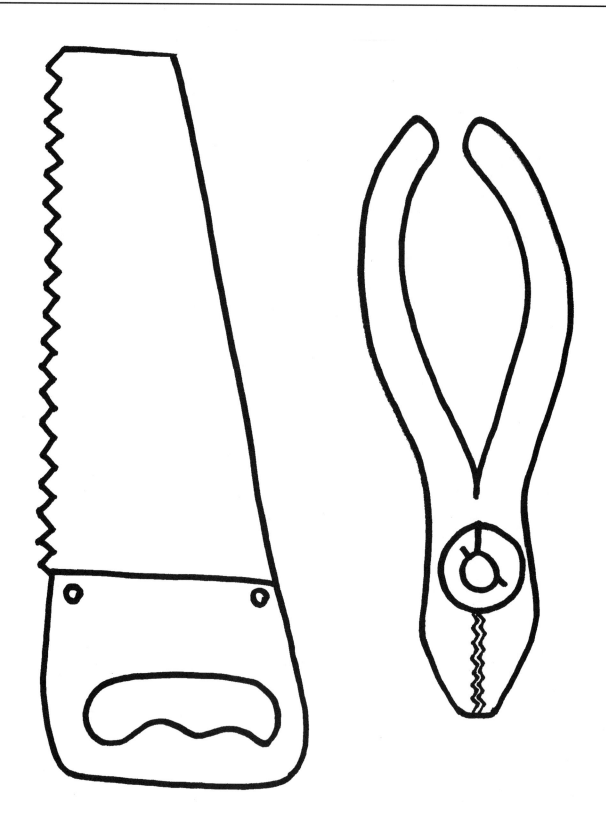

Figure 6.20 Toolbelt Patterns for "Who's Getting Dressed?"

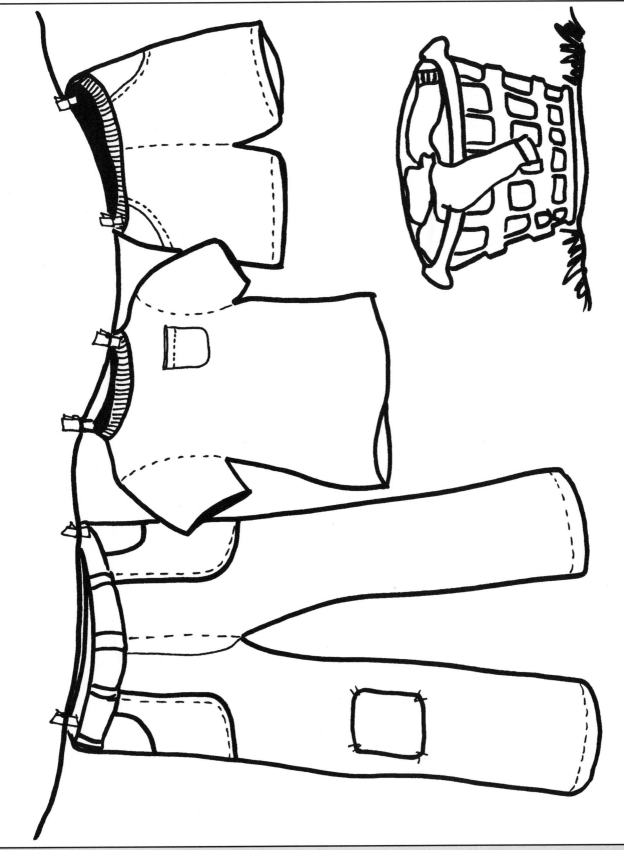

Figure 6.21 Clothesline Coloring Sheet

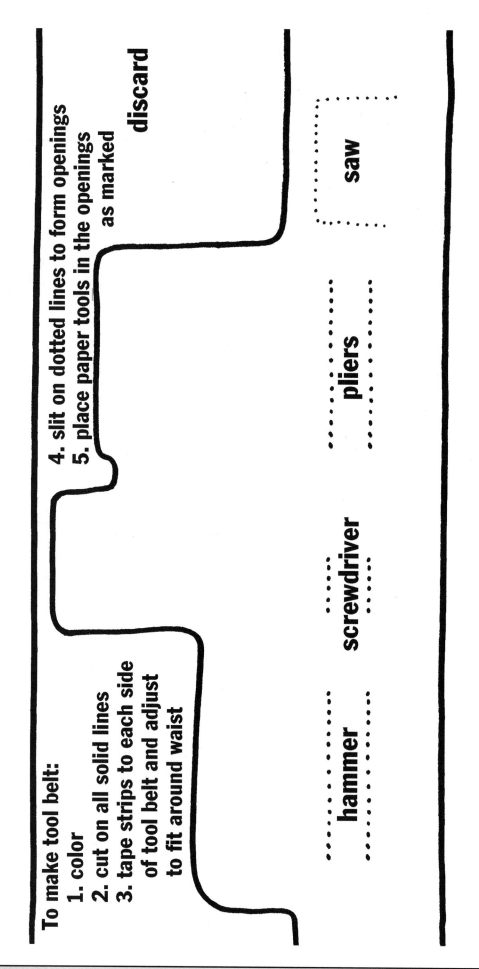

Figure 6.22 Toolbelt Activity Sheets

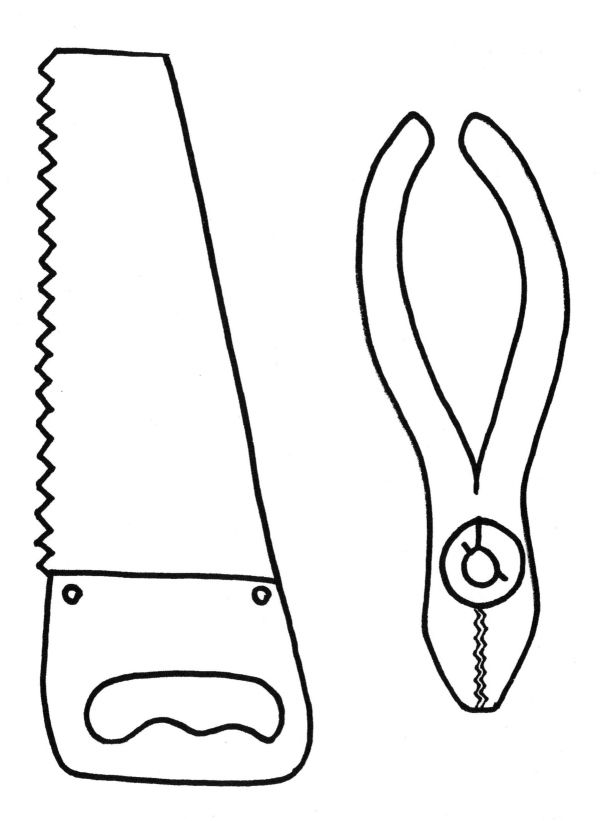

Figure 6.23 Toolbelt Activity Sheets

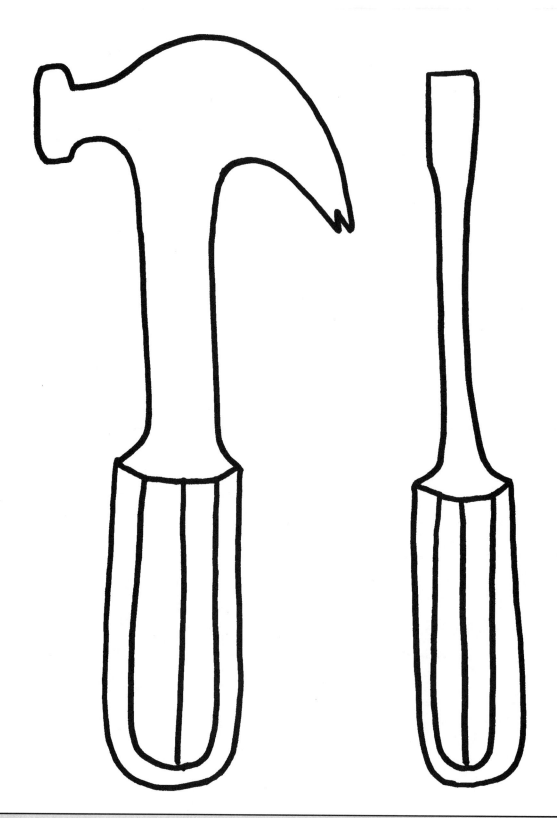

Figure 6.24 Toolbelt Activity Sheets

Index

About the Authors

GAIL BENTON AND TRISHA WAICHULAITIS have worked together providing storytimes at the City of Mesa Library for the past eleven years. Through this partnership they received the Sharon G. Womack Award in 1998, for sharing their ideas as presenters for the Arizona Library Association's Annual Conferences in 1993, 1995, 1996, and 1997. When not working at the library, Gail and Trisha continue to create and present workshops for the Arizona Reading Program, the Arizona Library Institute, and other library conferences. They also travel throughout Arizona presenting continuing education-funded workshops for the Arizona State Library.

Gail (left) and Trisha (right)